DOGS
AND THE LAW

By Anmarie Barrie, esq.

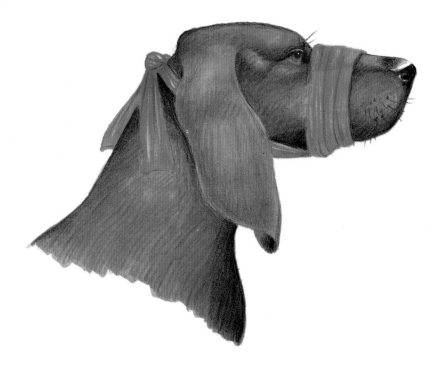

**The
illustration shows how a veterinarian would
muzzle a dog for temporary restraint.**

DOGS
AND THE LAW

By Anmarie Barrie, Esq.

CONTENTS

CONTENTS

Humorous drawings by Andrew Prendimano. Illustrative art by John R. Quinn, Scott Boldt and P.D. Protsenko.

© Copyright 1990 by T.F.H. Publications, Inc.

Distributed in the UNITED STATES by T.F.H. Publications, Inc., One T.F.H. Plaza, Neptune City, NJ 07753; in CANADA to the Pet Trade by H & L Pet Supplies Inc., 27 Kingston Crescent, Kitchener, Ontario N2B 2T6; Rolf C. Hagen Ltd., 3225 Sartelon Street, Montreal 382 Quebec; in CANADA to the Book Trade by Macmillan of Canada (A Division of Canada Publishing Corporation), 164 Commander Boulevard, Agincourt, Ontario M1S 3C7; in ENGLAND by T.F.H. Publications Limited, Cliveden House/Priors Way/Bray, Maidenhead, Berkshire SL6 2HP, England; in AUSTRALIA AND THE SOUTH PACIFIC by T.F.H. (Australia) Pty. Ltd., Box 149, Brookvale 2100 N.S.W., Australia; in NEW ZEALAND by Ross Haines & Son, Ltd., 82 D Elizabeth Knox Place, Panmure, Auckland, New Zealand; in the PHILIPPINES by Bio-Research, 5 Lippay Street, San Lorenzo Village, Makati Rizal; in SOUTH AFRICA by Multipet Pty. Ltd., Box 235 New Germany, South Africa 3620. Published by T.F.H. Publications, Inc. Manufactured in the United States of America by T.F.H. Publications, Inc.

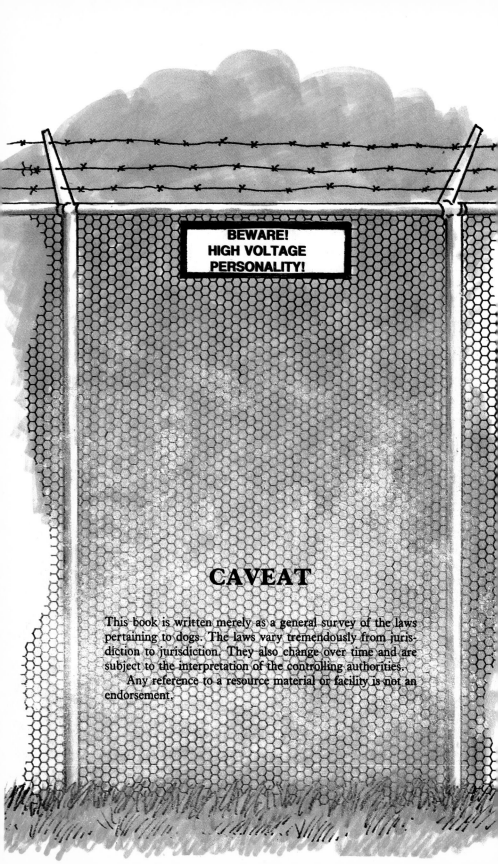

**BEWARE!
HIGH VOLTAGE
PERSONALITY!**

CAVEAT

This book is written merely as a general survey of the laws pertaining to dogs. The laws vary tremendously from jurisdiction to jurisdiction. They also change over time and are subject to the interpretation of the controlling authorities.

Any reference to a resource material or facility is not an endorsement.

The author, Anmarie Barrie, Esq., is a graduate of Seton Hall Law School in Newark, New Jersey.

She has written about a dozen books on pet animals and is currently employed by the Monmouth County Court System, Freehold, New Jersey.

This is *Tomarctus. Tomarctus* is
generally considered the
forerunner of dogs, wolves,
foxes and jackals.

History

No one knows for sure the exact origins of the dog. However, it is widely believed that dogs are descended from a family of carnivores (meat-eaters), the Miacidae, dating back 40 million years.

The Miacidae family had two descendants. One, called *Daphaenus*, gave rise to the bears. The other, *Cynodictis*, gave rise to a small, dog-like animal called *Tomarctus*. This is generally thought to be the forerunner of dogs, wolves, foxes and jackals.

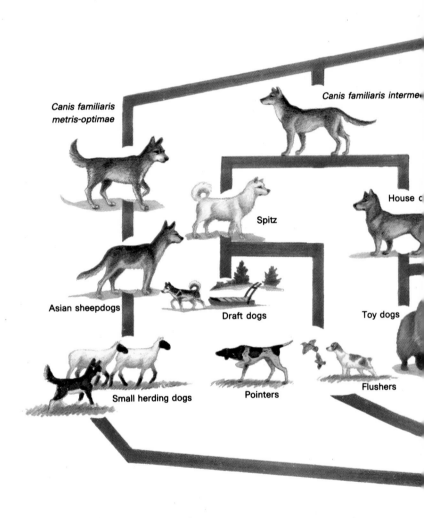

Canis familiaris metris-optimae

Canis familiaris interme

House

Spitz

Asian sheepdogs

Draft dogs

Toy dogs

Small herding dogs

Pointers

Flushers

THE FAMILY TREE OF THE EVOLUTION OF THE DOG

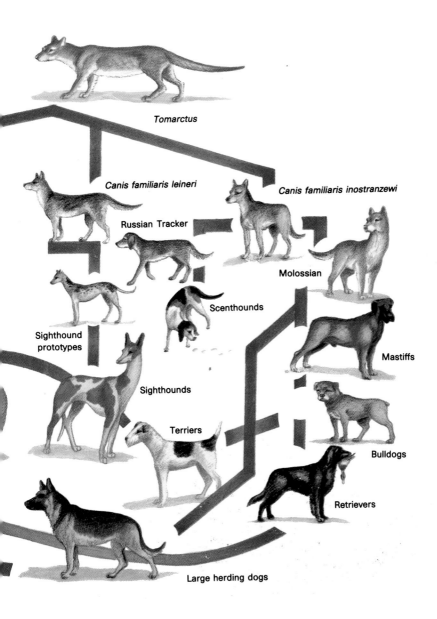

Tomarctus

Canis familiaris leineri

Canis familiaris inostranzewi

Russian Tracker

Molossian

Scenthounds

Sighthound prototypes

Mastiffs

Sighthounds

Terriers

Bulldogs

Retrievers

Large herding dogs

Dogs, wolves, foxes and jackals all belong to the family Canidae. Previously, it was commonly believed that the wolf or the jackal was the ancestor of the dog. Today, some authorities believe that although the three animals are related, they are separate offshoots of Tomarctus.

Stories and drawings of dogs appear on rock and papyrus as early as 3000 B.C. Bones of dogs have been found from even earlier years. Based on fossilized remains, the date for a type of prehistoric dog living domestically can be approximated. That date is placed between 6000 and 3000 B.C.

People and Dogs

Humans and dogs have been together since long before recorded history. We can only speculate about their first association. Now, however, it seems that where there are people, there are dogs. Dogs are found roaming the city streets, herding livestock, guarding property, hunting game, leading the blind, acting as ears for the deaf, and sniffing for drugs

People and dogs have lived and worked together for thousands of years. This Labrador Retriever is bringing a Mallard Duck back from the middle of a lake so a hunter may eat it.

Of all the many domesticated animals, only the dog becomes a companion, working pet. Dogs are easily trained and naturally friendly to their owners.

and explosives. Dogs have served in battle and now serve the disabled, the sick, and the old, and provide therapy to the emotionally disturbed. Mainly dogs seem to be kept for companionship and pleasure. Other animals are kept as pets, but none of them display the devotion, affection, eagerness, and intelligence of the dog.

As civilization advances and living conditions become more crowded, laws are created to keep society functioning smoothly. Our lives become more regulated, and this includes how we care for our dogs.

Laws dealing with this country's 52.4 million dogs are found at the federal, state and municipal levels of government. Mostly, though, dog law is a local affair. There are so many laws, and they vary so much from region to region, that it would be impractical to address them all in this book. However, there are general rules and guidelines that can be discussed. This book will teach you how to research and utilize the laws relevant to your particular area.

Throwing a Gumadisc, which is a soft Frisbee-type toy with a bone on top so it can be picked up by the dog, is normal behavior for both dog and owner. But is it legal? Someone might get hurt by the Frisbee-type toy, or the dog might invade private property to retrieve it. If you are concerned, learn how to do legal research.

Legal Research

It is usually the dog's mouth that gets him into trouble with the law. Biting, barking, tearing up furniture and whining for food when you are eating, can usually be prevented with proper training. In almost all cases, poor training and not the dog is responsible. If you own a dog, you are responsible for its behavior.

15

Legal research is like most other historical research. If you want to know how a dog evolved, you would look in the library or call an expert. The same is true of most legal research...start at the library first.

Legal Research

Legal research can be as easy as going to a public library, law school library, or public courthouse library. For federal laws, read the United States Constitution, federal statutes (laws passed by Congress), and federal case law (decisions rendered by the federal courts).

For state law, refer to your State Constitution, state law (laws passed by the state legislature), and state case law (decisions rendered by the state court). Finding out about city ordinances (laws enacted by the city council and county boards) is usually as simple as opening a three-ring binder and reading the entries under "Dogs." These municipal codes are often found at the city clerk's or city attorney's office. Sometimes a simple legal question can be answered by the humane society, animal control center, department of health, or local pet shop.

When looking for a statute, ordinance, or case, it should be easy to find if you have a citation (a reference). Usually, statutes are merely numbered and listed in order. Ky. Rev. Stat. §258.275 refers to the Kentucky Revised Statutes, section 258.275. Since the title of the statute book is abbreviated in a citation, the abbreviations and full titles of federal and state codes are given in Appendix A.

California, New York, Texas, and Maryland arrange their statutes into subject codes, such as Civil, Education, Penal, etc. Then the subject codes are arranged numerically. For example Cal. Civ. Code §3342, refers to the California Civil Code, section 3342. A list of the subject codes of these four states and their abbreviations is provided in Appendix B.

A case citation may look like this:

Henkel v. Jordan, 7 Kan.App.2d 561, 644 P.2d 1348, 30 A.L.R.4th 978 (1982).

Do not be intimidated. Even though this citation may seem complex at first glance, it is really quite simple. *Henkel v. Jordan* is the title of the case. Typically, the title names the parties involved in the dispute. In this case, Henkel is the plaintiff and Jordan is the defendant.

Three cites are listed, which means that the case is published in three reference works. Kan.App.2d is the abbreviation for the second edition of the books named the Kansas Court of Appeals Reports. The case is found in volume 7, beginning at page 561. P.2d is the short form of the Pacific Reporter, second edition. The case is printed in volume 644, beginning at page 1348. The third reference book that contains the case is the A.L.R.4th, or the fourth edition of the American Law Reports. Look on page 978 in volume 30. The case was decided in 1982.

You do not have to read the case in all three works. A citation merely lists all the reference books that contain the case as a matter of convenience; not all reference works are found in one library.

Case citations always abbreviate the title of the reference work. Therefore, Appendix C is a list of abbreviations of case books you are most likely to encounter in your research. Next to the abbreviation is the full title of the reference work.

The National Reporter System

The National Reporter System publishes reported decisions of all the states. Each state is not listed in its own volume; rather, the states are split into seven divisions. For each division of states, there is a set of volumes, called a reporter, containing the case law of all those states. Listed below are the seven National Reporters and the states contained within them.

Atlantic Reporter　　　(A., A2d)
　　Connecticut
　　Delaware
　　District of Columbia
　　Maine
　　Maryland
　　New Hampshire
　　New Jersey
　　Pennsylvania
　　Rhode Island
　　Vermont

North Eastern Reporter　　　(N.E., N.E.2d)
　　Illinois
　　Indiana
　　Massachusetts
　　New York
　　Ohio

North Western Reporter (N.W., N.W.2d)
　　Iowa
　　Michigan
　　Minnesota
　　Nebraska
　　North Dakota
　　South Dakota
　　Wisconsin

Pacific Reporter　　　(P., P.2d)
　　Alaska
　　Arizona
　　California
　　Colorado
　　Hawaii
　　Idaho
　　Kansas
　　Montana

Nevada
New Mexico
Oklahoma
Oregon
Utah
Washington
Wyoming

South Eastern Reporter (S.E., S.E.2d)
Georgia
North Carolina
South Carolina
Virginia
West Virginia

Southern Reporter (So., So.2d)
Alabama
Florida
Louisiana
Mississippi

South Western Reporter (S.W., S.W.2d)
Arkansas
Kentucky
Missouri
Tennessee
Texas

State Reports

Most states used to publish a series of books, called reports, that contained court decisions only of their state. Many states, though, have abandoned this practice and are listed only in the National Reporter System. The states that currently publish their own reports are listed below. All states, whether or not they have their own reference work, are included in the National Reporter System.

State	Full Title of Reference	Abbreviation
Alabama	Alabama Reports	Ala.
	Alabama Appellate Court Reports	Ala. App.
Alaska	Alaska Reports	Alaska
Arizona	Arizona Reports	Ariz.
Arkansas	Arkansas Reports	Ark.
California	California Reports	Cal., Cal.2d, Cal.3d
	California Appellate Reports	Cal.App., Cal.App.2d, Cal.App.3d
	West's California Reporter	Cal.Rptr.
Colorado	Colorado Reports	Colo.
	Colorado Court of Appeals Reports	Colo.App.
Connecticut	Connecticut Reports	Conn.
	Connecticut Supplement	Conn.Supp.
Delaware	Delaware Reports	Del.
Florida	Florida Reports	Fla.
	Florida Supplement	Fla.Supp.
Georgia	Georgia Reports	Ga.
	Georgia Appeals Reports	Ga.App.
Hawaii	Hawaii Reports	Hawaii
Idaho	Idaho Reports	Idaho
Illinois	Illinois Reports	Ill., Ill.2d
	Illinois Appellate Court Reports	Ill.App., Ill.App.2d, Ill.App.3d
Indiana	Indiana Reports	Ind.
	Indiana Court of Appeals Reports	Ind.App.
Iowa	Iowa Reports	Iowa
Kansas	Kansas Reports	Kan.
	Kansas Court of Appeals Reports	Kan.App.
Kentucky	Kentucky Reports	Ky.
Louisiana	Louisiana Reports	La.
Maine	Maine Reports	Me.
Maryland	Maryland Reports	Md.

	Maryland Appellate Reports	Md.App.
Massachusetts	Massachusetts Reports	Mass.
	Massachusetts Appeals Court Reports	Mass.App.Ct.
	Appellate Decisions	Mass.App.Dec.
Michigan	Michigan Reports	Mich.
Minnesota	Minnesota Reports	Minn.
Mississippi	Mississippi Reports	Miss.
Missouri	Missouri Reports	Mo.
	Missouri Appeals Reports	Mo.App.
Montana	Montana Reports	Mont.
Nebraska	Nebraska Reports	Neb.
Nevada	Nevada Reports	Nev.
New Hampshire	New Hampshire Reports	N.H.
New Jersey	New Jersey Reports	N.J.
	New Jersey Superior Court Reports	N.J.Super.
New Mexico	New Mexico Reports	N.M.
New York	New York Reports	N.Y., N.Y.2d
	West's New York Supplement	N.Y.S., N.Y.S.2d
	Appellate Division Reports	A.D., A.D.2d
	New York Miscellaneous Reports	Misc., Misc.2d
North Carolina	North Carolina Reports	N.C.
	North Carolina Court of Appeals Reports	N.C.App.
North Dakota	North Dakota Reports	N.D.
Ohio	Ohio State Reports	Ohio St., Ohio St.2d
	Ohio Appellate Reports	Ohio App., Ohio App.2d
	Ohio Miscellaneous	Ohio Misc.
	Ohio Opinions	Ohio Op., Ohio Op.2d, Ohio Op.3d
Oklahoma	Oklahoma Reports	Okla.
Oregon	Oregon Reports	Or.
	Oregon Reports, Court of Appeals	Or.App.
Pennsylvania	Pennsylvania State Reports	Pa.

	Pennsylvania Superior Court Reports	Pa.Super.
Rhode Island	Rhode Island Reports	R.I.
South Carolina	South Carolina Reports	S.C.
South Dakota	South Dakota Reports	S.D.
Tennessee	Tennessee Reports	Tenn.
	Tennessee Appeals	Tenn.App.
Texas	Texas Reports	Tex.
Utah	Utah Reports	Utah
Vermont	Vermont Reports	Vt.
Virginia	Virginia Reports	Va.
Washington	Washington Reports	Wash., Wash.2d
	Washington Appellate Reports	Wash.App.
West Virginia	West Virginia Reports	W.Va.
Wisconsin	Wisconsin Reports	Wis.,Wis.2d
Wyoming	Wyoming Reports	Wy.

The National Reporter System provides the volumes for New York (N.Y.S.) and California (West's California Reporter).

Indices and Digests

If you do not have a citation, then you must refer to the statute index. An index is a list of topics, arranged alphabetically, which are fully or partially covered by the particular set of reference books. Listed with topics are the statute numbers relevant to the heading. Research several topic headings (such as Dogs, Animals, etc.) until you find what you need. Each set of reference books will have its own index.

Some libraries will have an annotated book of statutes. This reference contains summaries of pertinent cases interpreting and applying the relevant statute.

If you do not have a citation when looking for case law, first look in the annotated statute book. If this book is not available, refer to a digest. This is a reference book arranged by headings. Under each heading is a compilation of case summations. If you have trouble finding a proper heading, refer to the index.

Use the Most Recent Citations

Read the most recent cases and statutes you can find. Laws cited in an older case or statute may not be valid anymore. Therefore, when using any reference work, check the pocket part or the supplement. The pocket part is a softcover pamphlet, inserted in the front or back cover of the book. A supplement is a soft-cover book located either next to the individual volume or at the end of the particular set of reference works. Since pocket parts and supplements are updated annually, they contain the most recent law.

Legal Definitions

Cases and statutes may include unfamiliar legal language. Or, a seemingly common word or phrase may have a precise and surprising legal definition. It is important to use a word or phrase in its proper legal context. Therefore, look up definitions in a legal dictionary, not merely a standard dictionary. Unlike most standard dictionaries, a legal dictionary defines phrases as well as words.

A seemingly common word may have a surprising legal definition.

Periodicals are useful resource guides.

There is no better place to discover how a term is applied in your jurisdiction than to read the relevant case law. Analyze how a word or phrase is interpreted in several cases to be sure that you have a sound understanding.

Other Reference Sources

Special programs for legal research, Lexis® and Westlaw®, are available on computer. Some libraries have these computer facilities. However, a fee may be involved. If you want some work done on the computer, you must do thorough research first. Information put into the computer must be precise. The more precise it is, the less time spent on the computer and the lower the cost.

Periodicals are useful resource guides. Newspapers and magazines provide an abundance of information about many topics dealing with dogs. They often discuss changes and trends in the law before the information is even available in official form.

Remember that the librarian is always willing to help you find what you need. Do not be afraid to ask.

Changing the Law

You may be dissatisfied with the laws of your state or municipality. Do not be disgruntled, but do your best to change them. You can advocate for new laws, or broaden, restrict, or eliminate existing laws by writing or lobbying your local representatives. Get the backing of other citizens and animal groups that support your views. With the help of an attorney, a law may be challenged in court.

If you leave your dog alone in a
motel room and he causes
extensive (or even minor)
damage, who do you think is
responsible? You're probably
right. The dog's owner is
responsible.

Owner Liability: Personal Injury; Property Damage; Nuisance

A dog's owner is legally
responsible, in most cases,
should his or her dog damage
the property of others.

28

Owner Liability: Personal Injury; Property Damage; Nuisance

An owner is legally responsible for controlling his dog. Most states make an owner legally liable for any personal injury or property damage (including killing livestock) caused by his pet. Depending upon the circumstances, an owner may be fined or jailed as well.

In addition, the owner will have to take measures designed to prevent further detriment. In serious cases, this could mean destruction of the dog. Therefore, a prudent owner will take precautionary measures designed to prevent his dog from causing harm. Given the right circumstances, any dog can injure or destroy.

Damages

If injury or damage occurs, an owner may have to pay medical expenses. This can include costs for doctors, hospitals, medications, physical therapy, and counseling. A victim may also be entitled to loss of earnings if he was out of work due to his injury. The time off may involve both treatment and recuperation.

Some courts may award compensation for pain and suffering experienced by the victim. The amount of the award can vary tremendously depending on the circumstance because it is difficult to calculate the cost specifically. Sometimes a spouse or close relative can receive compensation as well.

A dog's owner is usually responsible for a dog's behavior even though the owner is not at fault. The owner can be financially liable if his dog kills, maims, injures or even attacks livestock.

The theory is loss of service of the injured person. Loss of service is not limited to economics; it may include loss of companionship as well.

If the fault on the part of the owner is particularly shocking or reckless, a court may double or even triple the damage award. Additionally, the victim may be entitled to punitive damages. This recovery punishes the owner's poor conduct by making him pay even more than the amount considered adequate compensation to the victim. The financial status of the owner can be taken into account when establishing a punitive damage award.

Damages may be doubled if a guide dog is killed, wounded, or worried, or its blind owner is assaulted, bitten, or injured. R.I. Gen. Laws §4-13-16.1. The victim does not need to prove that the owner of the attacking dog knew of his pet's vicious nature.

A dog owner can be financially responsible if his dog kills, injures, or attacks livestock. Some states impose strict liability on the owner. This means that the owner is responsible for the dog's actions even though the owner is not at fault in any way. Some states have a fund that reimburses farmers or ranchers for damage done by dogs. Even if the farmer or rancher collects from the fund, he can still bring suit against the owner of the dog.

Legal Theories

There are several legal theories under which dog owners may be found liable for their dog's acts. One or more theories may be applicable in your state.

Many states have an on-duty exemption for trained police or military dogs. The police or government may be immune from liability if the injury occurred because the dog was provoked or while it was working. Cal. Civ. Code §3342(b); Mass. Gen. Laws Ann. §155A; Idaho Code §25-2808.

Dog Bite Statutes

Bite cases are the most common suit for which damages

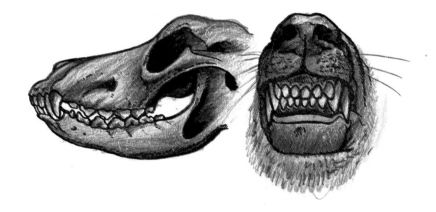

Dog bite cases are the most common legal actions brought against dog owners. Dogs have a full set of cutting, gripping and grinding teeth. Every year 10-20 people die from dog bites and many state laws hold the owner responsible, regardless of fault. That may mean that a thief, trespassing through your property, could sue you if he is attacked and wounded by your guard dog.

are brought. In 1985, 15 accidental deaths were the result of dog bites, according to the National Safety Council. Bites and attacks by dogs can be deadly as well as maiming. Therefore, many states have statutes that impose absolute liability, regardless of fault, on the owner for any injury or damage caused by his pet. Although these laws are referred to as dog bite statutes, they cover all types of dog-related injuries, not just bites.

Appendix D lists those states that have some type of dog bite statute and gives a sampling of the law. Not all of the dog bite statutes are listed. As Appendix D shows, dog bite statutes are listed under an assortment of titles, including torts, licenses, agriculture, animals, nuisance, etc. The related dog bite topics covered by the statutes, such as damages, hearings, penalties, and livestock funds, vary widely from state to state.

An injured person often sues under a dog bite statute because, if the statute is applicable, liability is automatic. This means that the victim does not have to prove that the owner did anything wrong if the circumstances of the injury are covered by the statute. Strict liability may be imposed regardless of whether or not the owner was careless, tried to prevent injury, or was unaware that the dog was dangerous.

Read the statute carefully. The injured party must show that all the elements required by the law have been met. In some states, the burden of proof is on the owner to prove that he was not at fault. Other statutes shift the burden of proof to the victim; he must prove that he was not at fault.

The elements covered by a dog bite statute typically include the type of injury, the place of the event, who can sue, who can be sued, defenses, and actions of the victim. For example, the injury may be limited to bites, or it may cover other types of damage. Often it is only the injured party that can sue. In some states, the victim can sue the owner as well as the keeper of the animal. For the injured party to prevail, he may have to prove that he was in a public place, lawfully on private property, or he may have to have been on the owner's property at the time of the attack. A statute may list the defenses available to the dog owner, such as provocation or assumption of risk by the victim.

Let's take a look at the New Jersey statute: The owner of any dog which shall bite a person while such person is on or in a public place, or lawfully on or in a private place, including the property of the owner of the dog, shall be liable for such damages as may be suffered by the person bitten, regardless of the former viciousness of such dog or the owner's knowledge of such viciousness. For the purpose of this section, a person is lawfully upon the private property of such owner when he is on the property in the performance of any duty imposed upon him by the laws of this state or the laws or postal regulation of the United States, or when he is on such property upon the invitation, express or implied, of the owner thereof. N.J. Stat. Ann. §4:19-16.

According to the New Jersey statute, the parties are limited to the victim and the dog owner. The injury is restricted to a dog bite, and the victim must prove he was damaged. The event does not have to take place on the owner's property; the victim can be on public property, or lawfully on private property. (The statute defines what constitutes a lawful presence on private property.) The owner is not excused from liability because he was unaware of the dog's vicious nature. However, the owner is not barred from raising the defenses of provocation, negligence, trespass, or assumption of risk.

When evaluating a statute, do not limit yourself to a literal reading. It is important to research the case decisions because the court may have a different interpretation of the law than you do. For example, a statute often uses a term, such as owner, but does not define it. You may assume that the owner is the person with legal title. However, the definition of an owner as determined in the case law may be broad enough to include the legal owner, as well as anyone who cares for, harbors, or has custody of the dog.

Another example is that case law may restrict an owner's

A dog's owner is not free from liability because he did not know his dog was vicious. However, he might defend himself (and his dog) by raising the defenses of provocation, negligence, trespass, or assumption of risk (i.e., the injured party knew the dog was nasty, but thought he could pet him anyway).

defenses even though the statute does not. Arizona's statute reads: "Injury to any person or damage to any property by a dog while at large shall be the full responsibility of the dog owner or person or persons responsible for the dog when such damages were inflicted." Ariz. Rev. Stat. Ann. §24-378.

According to the statute, the owner is not limited in the defenses he can raise. However, the case law reveals that assumption of risk is not available as a defense. In fact, the only defense he can plead is provocation of the dog by the victim. *Massey v. Colaric*, 151 Ariz. 65, 725 P.2d 1099 (1986). So, for a thorough analysis, your legal research must encompass the case law as well as the statutory law.

Common Law Rules

Common law is law garnered from case decisions; it is not codified in statutes or ordinances. Under the common law developed by the courts, there exists the one bite rule. This rule allows a dog not necessarily a free bite, but one chance to exhibit dangerous behavior before its owner is legally responsible for injury caused by the dog. Hence, an owner is on notice that the dog is prone to bite or otherwise cause injury. Sometimes the common law language uses the term "vicious." This just means likely to hurt someone; it does not refer to the dog's overall temperament.

For instance, a dog owner knew his dog "Peanut" had a menacing behavior toward people. As a cyclist was riding past the yard of the dog owner, the dog rushed forward and began to bark in a threatening manner. The cyclist lost control of the bike, fell, and sustained injury. Since the owner knew the dog had a menacing behavior toward people, he was held accountable for the dog's actions. Even though such knowledge might not be sufficient to impose liability for a bite, it was sufficient in this case because it was the dog's menacing behavior that caused the injury. It did not matter that Peanut weighed less than 20 pounds. *Henkel v. Jordan*, 7 Kan.App.2d 561, 644 P.2d 1348, 30 A.L.R.4th 978 (1982).

In states with dog bite statutes, an injured person can still sue under the common law if the statute does not cover the particular circumstances. However, under the common law, the victim must prove that the owner was aware of the dog's propensity to cause harm.

Negligence

If the situation does not fall within the dog bite statute, and the victim cannot prove that the owner knew of the dog's dangerousness, there is another legal theory. If the injured party can show that the owner was unreasonably careless in controlling the dog, compensation may be awarded for harm that was reasonably foreseeable as a result. If a court determines that a dog owner acted reasonably under the circumstances, though, there is no negligence. Violation of a law, such as a leash law, may be negligence per se; the victim need only prove that the owner was in breach.

Nuisance

A dog may not have caused physical damage or injury, but it may be a nuisance. A nuisance can be characterized as anything which repeatedly causes a substantial and unreasonable or unlawful annoyance, disturbance, inconvenience or damage to another. For instance, a dog that barks incessantly or late at night may be a nuisance. An unlicensed dog, Ann. Ind. Code §15-5-9-14, or a dog running at large, S.D. Codified Laws Ann. §40-34-4, may be a nuisance. For an owner that lives in an apartment, a dog deemed a nuisance can be sufficient grounds for an owner to be sued or evicted.

A Special Note About Mail Carriers

Postal workers are probably the most frequent victims of dog attacks. A dog owner must be sure that his dog cannot interrupt the letter carrier's job in any way. If a postal employee is injured by a dog, the postal service can pursue collection for all damages, including lost wages, medical costs, and damage to personal property and clothing. The postal sevice can file municipal complaints against a dog owner who fails to control his animal properly.

Defenses

The owner has some defenses that he can plead. The defenses acceptable in a court vary from state to state. In addition, the right to declare a particular defense may be governed by the legal theory asserted by the injured party. For instance, contributory negligence may be an acceptable defense against an attack under the common law, but it may be barred as a defense against a dog bite statute.

Negligence

The owner may offer proof of contributory or comparative negligence on the part of the victim. This means that the injured party displayed conduct falling below that of a reasonable person. He was bitten, at least partly, due to his own careless behavior. For example, a person can be found negligent if he trespasses on private property, ignores "Beware of Dog" signs, or teases the dog. Contributory negligence is a complete bar to recovery. The doctrine of comparative negligence reduces the amount of the award the victim can collect.

Assumption of Risk

The owner may escape liability by asserting assumption of risk by the victim. In this situation, the victim may not recover for damages if he voluntarily exposes himself to a known and appreciated danger. The owner must prove that the injured party had knowledge of the facts, knew of the dangerous condition, appreciated the nature and extent of the risk, and voluntarily exposed himself to it. This is one situation when posting a "Beware of Dog" sign may come into play. Also, veterinarians and staff members bitten when treating a dog may have assumed the risk. They knew of the danger and acted deliberately in treating the dog.

Provocation

Another defense is intentional provocation of the dog by the victim. Here, the injured party acted purposefully in irritating, inciting, or arousing rage in the dog. Provocation does not have to be deliberate. For example, someone may accidentally step on a dog's tail. A court may consider that a veterinarian, in his treatment of a dog, provoked it to bite. An owner, though, cannot conceal the fact that his dog is dangerous.

Unlawful Acts

In some states, a victim engaged in an unlawful act at the time of the injury may not recover anything from the dog owner. A statute may require the victim to prove he was not breaking the law; the owner does not have to prove the victim was doing an illegal act. If the victim cannot prove his good conduct, there is no recovery.

Trespassing

Some states do not protect trespassers who are injured by a dog. A trespasser is someone on your property who has not been invited. However, an invitation does not have to be explicit; it can be implied. Anyone that you can reasonably expect to be on your property, such as a delivery person or mail carrier, has an implied invitation, unless warnings are posted to the contrary.

According to a literal reading of the common law, a dog owner who knew of his dog's dangerous propensity would be liable for injuries sustained by a trespasser. Many courts modify the doctrine to avoid unfairness. Recovery is denied if the victim is a trespasser, or a trespasser may not receive compensation if the dog is a guard dog.

Some courts permit an owner to raise the defenses of contributory or comparative negligence, or assumption of the risk against the claims of a trespasser. The trespasser may be allowed to show that the owner acted unreasonably under the circumstances.

Some states permit a trespasser to sue only if the landowner knew that the intruder was on the property. The landowner is responsible only if he knew of the intruder's presence, and intentionally caused harm or failed to warn of danger.

In particular, children often are deemed to have an implied invitation to enter property. Children do not possess the reasoning capabilities of adults. Therefore, an adult bears a heavy burden of protecting children from a dog.

Statute of Limitations

Different legal theories have different statutes of limitations (time limits). These statutes establish a particular time in which suit must be brought. For example, a dog bite statute may require a suit to be filed within one year from the date of the injury; a suit brought under the common law theory may have a two-year limit. Check the laws of your jurisdiction. If you intend to sue, file the action as soon as possible to avoid dismissal on the grounds that the statute of limitations has run out.

Preventing Injury

If you are a dog owner, the best way to avoid liability is to prevent injury. Adhere to a few common sense rules to keep risk of harm to a minimum.

No matter how small, old or timid your dog is, it can hurt someone, damage property, or be a nuisance. Any dog may bite or scratch if it is threatened, or if it is protecting its owner, its puppies, or its food. A dog racing around a corner or barking unexpectedly may startle an unsuspecting person which can result in injury.

Therefore, keep your dog securely contained in the house or yard. Be sure it cannot escape to scare or otherwise get in the way of strangers. Post warning signs that alert passersby that a dog is present. Never let your dog off its leash to run at large. The owner must be in control at all times.

Lastly, keep the dog's license and vaccinations up-to-date. If your dog does manage to get free, its return will be more expedient if it is properly identified. The less time out of your care, the less time the dog has to cause trouble. And should the dog bite someone, the dog will not need to be quarantined if its rabies vaccine is current.

Responsibility Rests With Owners and Keepers

Typically it is the dog's legal owner that is responsible for the actions of his pet. However, someone else, or more than one person, may be liable. For instance, a dog may have more than one owner, or someone other than the owner may have custody of the dog.

A keeper is a person who cares for, manages, or possesses a dog. Often the owner and the keeper are the same person, but sometimes they are not. A state may establish that the keeper is responsible, or it may determine that both the owner and the keeper are liable. Some states strictly limit responsibility to the owner.

A dog owner may be under 18 years of age. In such a situation, the minor's parents or legal guardian may be responsible for any injury or damage caused by the dog. A court may impose liability under one of several legal theories. The parents may be considered the keepers of the dog; they may be deemed responsible for damage caused by their minor child; or a statute may expressly state that the parents of a minor are responsible for the dog. R.I. Gen. Laws §4-13.1-14.

Under certain circumstances, liability may be imposed on a landlord. The landlord must have known that a tenant's dog was dangerous, and he must have been capable of removing the dog, but did nothing about it. A landlord who knows that a tenant has a vicious dog must take reasonable measures to protect people who might be on the premises from being attacked by the dog. Precautionary provisions may be included in the lease. *Strunk v. Zoltanski*, 62 N.Y.2d 572, 468 N.E.2d 13, 479 N.Y.S.2d 175 (1984).

Insurance

The cost of the potential damage and injury inflicted by a dog can be enormous. A wise owner will check to see that his homeowner's or renter's policy covers his dog. A dog that exhibits menacing behavior should have its own insurance coverage.

A typical homeowner's or renter's insurance plan covers any damage caused by the policy holder's negligence. This coverage often extends to incidents that take place away from the owner's property, even if a vehicle is involved. If the policy does not extend to vehicular events, look to your auto insurance plan. Some insurance companies refuse to issue a policy altogether if a vicious dog lives in the home.

Often a plan limits its coverage to the first instance of harm caused by a dog. After that, the owner must pay out of his own pocket. Other companies exclude certain types of dog-related harm from their coverage. This is why it is important to read your policy carefully. If you do not understand the terms, call your agent for an explanation. It is important to know your liability before an accident occurs.

If your home and auto insurance do not extend to dog-related injuries, or you think the coverage is not broad enough, buy insurance for your pet. If you own a pit bull or another potentially vicious dog, the law might require you to have such a policy. Take out insurance that will protect you and the dog while at home and away. Get a policy that will pay for your dog's medical expenses as well.

Guide dogs are trained to act as eyes for the visually impaired (blind). The dog must graduate from a rigorous training program. Then the dog is matched with his owner. Small dogs are almost never chosen as guide or Seeing Eye dogs.

Assistance Dogs

Assistance Dogs

There are several types of assistance dogs which bring independence to the lives of the disabled. Guide dogs aid the visually impaired; signal dogs work for the hearing impaired; service dogs function as the arms or legs of the physically challenged; therapy dogs provide social and therapy functions for an individual or in a variety of institutions; and specialty dogs are custom-trained to meet the needs of an individual who does not fit neatly into one of the other categories.

Getting a guide, signal, specialty, or service dog is a lot like adopting a child. The dog must graduate from a rigorous training program. Then the dog is matched with its new owner. The pair must pass a series of written and working tests before they are allowed to go home together. The owner and the dog develop a special, working partnership that lasts for many years.

Guide Dogs

Guide dogs are trained to act as eyes for the visually impaired. The dog stops at curbs, steers around obstacles, and identifies overhanging awnings and signs that could be harmful to its owner. The term guide dog is the generic name, but the dogs are also referred to as guide dogs, Seeing Eye dogs, and dog leaders. Systematic schooling began in Germany around 1916.

For more information about guide dogs, contact the following organizations.

Alaska SPCA
3439 East Tudor Road
Anchorage, AK 99502

Auger's Animal and Dog Training Ltd.
90 Ramapo Valley Road
Oakland, NJ 07436
(201) 337-6179

Canine Working Companions for
  Independence
RD 2, Box 170
Gorton Lake Road
Waterville, NY 13480
(315) 861-7770 (Voice or TDD)

Guide Dog Association of
  New South Wales
P.A.T. Training Center
77 Deepfield Road
Catherine Field
NSW 2171 Sydney, Australia
02-606-6616

Guide Dogs for the Blind
P.O. Box 1200
San Rafael, CA 94915
(415) 479-4000

Guide Dogs of the Desert
P.O. Box 1692
Palm Springs, CA 92263
(619) 329-6257

Inner Sight for the Blind
944 Manor Road
Staten Island, NY 10314

Leader Dogs for the Blind
1039 Rochester Road
Rochester, MI 48063
(313) 651-9011

Southeastern Guide Dogs
4120 77th Street East
Palmetto, FL 33561
(813) 729-5665

Animals for Independence and Mobility
11071 East Stanley Road
Davison, MI 48423
(313) 653-3842

Canine Helpers for the Handicapped
5699–5705 Ridge Road (Rt. 104)
Lockport, NY 14094
(716) 433-4035 (Voice or TTY)

Fidelco Guide Dog Foundation
P.O. Box 142
Bloomfield, CT 06002
(203) 243-5200

Guide Dog Foundation for the Blind
371 East Jericho Turnpike
Smithtown, NY 11787
(516) 265-2121

Guide Dogs for the Blind Association
9, 10, 11 Park Street
Windsor, Berkshire, SL4 1JR
Great Britain

Guiding Eyes for the Blind
611 Granite Springs Road
Yorktown Heights, NY 10598
(914) 245-4024

International Guiding Eyes
13445 Glenoaks Boulevard
Sylmar, CA 91342
(818) 362-5834

Pilot Dogs
625 West Town Street
Columbus, OH 43215
(614) 221-6367

The Seeing Eye Dog
P.O. Box 375
Morristown, NJ, 07960
(201) 539-4425

Signal Dogs

Signal dogs, also known as hearing dogs, are taught general obedience, as well as how to respond to sounds. Typical sounds include an alarm clock, doorbell, fire alarm, telephone, a baby crying, and a falling object. The dog alerts its hearing impaired owner by making physical contact and leading him to the source of the sound.

For more information about signal dogs, contact the following organizations.

American Humane Association's Center
for Hearing Dogs
9725 East Hampden Avenue
Denver, CO 80231
(303) 695-0811

Animals for Independence and Mobility
11071 East Stanley Road
Davison, MI 48423
(313) 653-3842

Arlington Humane Society
7817 South Cooper Street
Arlington, TX 76017

Audio Dogs
27 Crescent Street
Brooklyn, NY 11208
(212) 827-2792

Auger's Animal and Dog Training Ltd.
90 Ramapo Valley Road
Oakland, NJ 07436
(201) 337-6179

Canine Companions for Independence
Executive Office
P.O. Box 446
Santa Rosa, CA 95402-0466
(707) 528-0830 (Voice or TDD)

Canine Helpers for the Handicapped
5699–5705 Ridge Road (Rt. 104)
Lockport, NY 14094
(716) 433-4035 (Voice or TTY)

Canine Working Companions
RD 2, Box 170
Gorton Lake Road
Waterville, NY 13480
(315) 861-7770 (Voice or TDD)

Connecticut K-9 Hearing Dog Training
239 Maple Hill Avenue
Newington, CT 06111
(203) 666-4646 (Voice)
(203) 666-4648 (TTY)

Dogs for the Deaf
13260 Highway 238
Jacksonville, OR 97530
(503) 899-7177 (Voice)
(503) 846-6783 (TTY)

Signal dogs, or hearing dogs, are
taught to respond to sounds
such as a fire alarm, a baby
crying, the doorbell or phone
ringing, and the like. The dog
alerts its deaf owner and leads
him to the source of the sound.

Dogs for Independence
P.O. Box 965
Ellenburg, WA 98926
(509) 925-4535

Dogs for Independent Living
P.O. Box 2055
Montrose, CO 81402

E.A.R. Foundation
Baptist Hospital—West Building
2000 Church Street
Nashville, TN 37236
(615) 327-4870

Ears for the Deaf
803 Carlton Street
Mishawaka, IN 46544

Ears for the Deaf
1235 100th Street, S.E.
Byron Center, MI 49315
(616) 698-0688

Ears for the Deaf of Florida
P.O. Box 9419
Bradenton, FL 34206
(813) 758-2539 (Voice or TTY)

Feeling Heart Foundation
RFD 2, Box 345
Cambridge, MD 21613
(301) 228-3689

Freedom Service Dogs
980 Everett Street
Lakewood, CO 80215
(303) 234-9512

Great Lakes Hearing Dog Program
5800 North Lovers Land Road
Milwaukee, WI 53201
(414) 463-8300 (Voice)
(414) 463-1990 (TTY)

Guide Dog Association of
    New South Wales
P.A.T. Training Center
77 Deepfield Road
Catherine Field
NSW 2171 Sydney, Australia
02-606-6616

Guide Dog Foundation for the
    Handicapped
118 Slade Avenue
Columbus, OH 43220
(614) 451-2969

Handi-Dogs
P.O. Box 12563
Tucson, AZ 85732
(603) 326-3412

Harken Hearing Dogs
165 Stein Road
Ann Arbor, MI 48105

Hearing Dog
5901 East 89th Avenue
Henderson, CO 80640
(303) 287-3277

Hearing Dogs in England
192 Burton Road
Melton, Mowbray LE13 1DN
Great Britain

Hearing Dogs for the Deaf
6940 48th Street
Coloma, MI 49038
(616) 468-6154

Hearing Dogs for the Deaf
London Road (A-40)
Lewknor, Oxford OX95RY
Great Britain

Hearing Ear Dog Program
P.O. Box 213
West Boylston, MA 01583
(617) 835-3304

Humane Society of Indianapolis
7929 North Michigan Road
Indianapolis, IN 46268

Iowa Hearing Dog Program
2258 Logan Avenue
Waterloo, IA 50703
(319) 236-2987

National Association for the Deaf
814 Thayer Avenue
Silver Spring, MD 20910
(301) 587-1788

Okada, Ltd.
P.O. RR #1
Fontana, WI 53125
(414) 275-5226

Pro-Dogs, The Dog House
Rocky Bank, 4. New Road, Ditton,
Maidstone, Kent MEZO 7AD
Great Britain

San Diego Dogs for the Deaf
P.O. Box 33191
San Diego, CA 92130-0400

Hearing Dogs of the South
998 Sousa Drive
Largo, FL 33541
(813) 530-4929

Hearing Dogs of New England
420 Groton Long Point Road
Groton, CT 06340
(203) 536-4849

International Hearing Dog, Inc.
5901 East 89th Avenue
Henderson, CO 80640
(303) 287-3277 (Voice or TTY)

Mary Ann Salem Companion Animal
   Program for the Deaf
Riverside Humane Society
5791 Fremont Street
Riverside, CA 92504
(714) 688-4340

National Hearing Aid Dog Training
   Association
402 West Patterson
Flint, MI 48503
(313) 767-4503

Paws to Listen
P.O. Box 855
South Bend, IN 46624
(219) 287-4273

Red Acre Farm Hearing Dog Center
Box 278
109 Red Acre Road
Stow, MA 01775
(508) 897-8343 (Voice or TTY)

San Francisco SPCA Hearing
   Dog Program
2500 16th Street
San Francisco, CA 94103
(415) 621-1700 (Voice)
(415) 621-2174 (TTY)

Society for Animal Protective
  Legislation
P.O. Box 3719
Georgetown Station
Washington, D.C. 20007

Speech Hearing and Learning Center
Southeastern Assistance Dogs
811 Pendleton Street
9-11 Medical Center
Greenville, SC 29601
(803) 235-9689

Western Canada's Handi & Hearing
  Dog Society
10060 #5 Road
Richmond, British Columbia
Canada V7A 4E5
(604) 277-3158

Southeast Hearing Dog Program
Baptist Hospital
Box 111
2000 Church Street
Nashville, TN 37236
(615) 329-7807

Working P.A.W.S.
P.O. Box 81
Wyatt, IN 46595
(219) 277-6525

Service Dogs

Service dogs, also known as mobility dogs, assist the physically challenged individual. A dog is taught many tasks, including turning light switches on and off, retrieving a variety of items, pulling a wheelchair, and pushing elevator buttons. The dog is also trained to open doors, pull on clothing, and drag its owner to safety.

For more information about service dogs, contact the following organizations.

Canine Companions for Independence
Executive Office
P.O. Box 446
Santa Rosa, CA 95402-0466
(707) 528-0830 (Voice or TDD)

Canine Helpers for the Handicapped
5699-5705 Ridge Road (Rt. 104)
Lockport, NY 14094
(716) 433-4035 (Voice or TTY)

Canine Working Companions
for Independence
RD 2, Box 170
Gorton Lake Road
Waterville, NY 13480
(315) 861-7770 (Voice or TDD)

Guide Dog Association of
New South Wales
P.A.T. Training Center
77 Deepfield Road
Catherine Field
NSW 2171 Sydney, Australia
02-606-6616

Guide Dogs for the Handicapped
118 Slade Avenue
Columbus, OH 43220
(614) 451-2969

Handi-Dogs
P.O. Box 12563
Tucson, AZ 85732
(603) 326-3412

Happy Canine Helpers
16277 Montgomery Road
Johnstown, OH 43031
(614) 965-2204

Helping Paws
Box 197 Mayo Building
University of Minnesota
Minneapolis, MN 55455
(612) 626-1051

Independence Dogs
258A RD 1, Maple Lane
Chadds Ford, PA 19317
(215) 358-2723

Nanhall Training Center
2206 Asheboro Street
Greensboro, NC 27406
(919) 272-6584

Prison Pet Partnership
Washington Correction Center for Women
P.O. Box 17, B27-21
Gig Harbor, WA 98335
(206) 858-9101

Support Dogs for the Handicapped
P.O. Box 966
St. Louis, MO 63128
(314) 739-3317

Western Canada's Handi and
Hearing Dog Society
10060 #5 Road
Richmond, British Columbia
Canada V7A 4E5
(604) 277-3158

Therapy Dogs

When people talk to people, their blood pressure rises. Yet when people talk to dogs, their blood pressure goes down. Dogs and humans relate so well because dogs give unconditional love and affection. This non-judgmental interaction has a therapeutic effect on disturbed, disabled, convalescing, or confined individuals. Caring for a dog raises morale and social activity, and actually gives some people a reason to live.

Therefore, an assortment of animals, including dogs, tropical fish, guinea pigs and other domestic pets, is used in a variety of therapy programs. Many health care facilities, including hospitals, day care centers, psychiatric wards, abuse shelters and nursing homes, with programs for the sick, the elderly, and the mentally disabled, utilize therapy or social dogs in their programs. Dogs are even allowed to visit prison inmates. Some institutions allow patients to have visits from their own household pets.

Laws are not required for a facility in your state to allow pets. There are no laws against such an activity. The decision is up to the administrators of the particular institution. An arrangement must be made between the institution and a facility that will provide the animals.

For more information about therapy dogs, contact the following organizations.

Canine Companions for Independence
Executive Office
P.O. Box 446
Santa Rosa, CA 95402-0466
(707) 528-0830 (Voice or TDD)

Canine Helpers for the Handicapped
5699-5705 Ridge Road (Rt. 104)
Lockport, NY 14094
(716) 433-4035 (Voice or TTY)

Specialty Dogs

Specialty dogs are individually trained to meet the needs of people with   special or a combination of disabilities. For example, a dog can be trained to aid a deaf person confined to a wheelchair.

For more information about specialty dogs, contact the following organizations.

Animals for Independence and Mobility
11071 East Stanley Road
Davison, MI 48423
(313) 653-3842

Canine Helpers for the Handicapped
5699-5705 Ridge Road (Rt. 104)
Lockport, NY 14094
(716) 433-4035 (Voice or TTY)

Dogs for Independence
P.O. Box 965
Ellenburg, WA 98926
(509) 925-4535

Freedom Service Dogs
980 Everett Street
Lakewood, CO 80215
(303) 234-9512

Guide Dogs for the Handicapped
118 Slade Avenue
Columbus, OH 43220
(614) 451-2969

Hearing Ear Dog Program
P.O. Box 213
West Boylston, MA 01583
(167) 835-3304

International Guiding Eyes
13445 Glenoaks Boulevard
Sylmar, CA 91342
(818) 362-5834

Iowa Hearing Dog Program
2258 Logan Avenue
Waterloo, IA 50703
(319) 236-2987

Canine Companions for Independence
Executive Office
P.O. Box 446
Santa Rosa, CA 95402-0466
(707) 528-0830 (Voice or TDD)

Canine Working Companions
   for Independence
RD 2, Box 170
Gorton Lake Road
Waterville, NY 13480
(315) 861-7770 (Voice or TDD)

Ears for the Deaf, Inc.
1235 100th Street, S.E.
Byron Center, MI 49315
(616) 698-0688

Guide Dog Association of
   New South Wales
P.A.T. Training Center
77 Deepfield Road
Catherine Field
NSW 2171 Sydney, Australia
02-606-6616

Handi-Dogs
P.O. Box 12563
Tucson, AZ 85732
(603) 326-3412

Hearing Dogs of the South
998 Sousa Drive
Largo, FL 33541
(813) 530-4929

International Hearing Dogs, Inc.
5901 East 89th Avenue
Henderson, CO 80640
(303) 287-3277 (Voice or TTY)

Okada, Ltd.
P.O. Box RR #1
Fontana, WI 53125
(414) 275-5226

Paws to Listen
P.O. Box 855
South Bend, IN 46624
(219) 287-4273

Red Acre Farm Hearing Dog Center
Box 278
109 Red Acre Road
Stow, MA 01775
(508) 897-8343 (Voice or TTY)

Southeast Hearing Dog Program
Baptist Hospital
Box 111
2000 Church Street
Nashville, TN 37236
(615) 329-7807

Speech Hearing and Learning Center
Southeastern Assistance Dogs
811 Pendleton Street
9-11 Medical Center
Greenville, SC 29601
(803) 235-9689

Support Dogs for the Handicapped
P.O. Box 966
St. Louis, MO 63128
(314) 739-3317

Western Canada's Handi and
   Hearing Dog Society
10060 #5 Road
Richmond, British Columbia
Canada V7A 4E5
(604) 277-3158

Working P.A.W.S.
P.O. Box 81
Wyatt, IN 46595
(219) 277-6525

Legal Status

Assistance dogs have a legally recognized status in many states. They have certain privileges that other dogs do not. For example, assistance dogs are often exempt from certain laws, such as pooper-scooper laws, N.Y. Pub. Health Law §1310, or a no-pets clause in a lease. A statute may or may not expressly state that assistance dogs are an exemption to the law. However, a court may choose not to enforce a restriction against an assistance dog even though there is no specific exception.

Not all assistance dogs receive the same privileged status, though. Some laws recognize only guide dogs, or only guide and service dogs, etc. So if you are trying to utilize the law,

Assistance dogs should always display a special dog tag.

be sure that your type of assistance dog is included in the rules.

If an owner has a problem taking advantage of the laws available to an assistance dog, a special dog tag should be displayed. It might be wise for the owner to carry around a copy of the laws exempting assistance dogs from the law and allowing them access to public facilities. People are quite impressed by the written law. If that does not work, volunteer to call the police. After all, the law is on the owner's side.

Federal and State

Assistance dogs can enter premises which exclude other animals. Buildings owned by the federal government admit entry to guide dogs. The dog owners are subject to the same regulations as other people. 40 U.S.C. §291.

State statutes such as N.Y. Civ. Rights Law §47 and Fla. Stat. §413.08 permit guide dogs in public facilities. Public property usually means anywhere the public is permitted; it does not just mean property owned by the government. This includes educational facilities, theaters, elevators, and modes of transportation. Additionally, it may be illegal for any person or legal entity, public or private, to impose an additional charge or other restriction when admitting a guide dog. N.Y. Civ. Rights Law §47b. Yet the dog owner is probably still liable for any damage his pet may cause. Cal. Civ. Code §54.2. A person who refuses to permit a guide dog to enter a public place may be guilty of a misdemeanor and fined. Ala. Code §3-1-7.

Other premises that must permit assistance dogs may include rental or public housing and the workplace. Although dogs are often banned from rental and public housing, many states consider it illegal to refuse accommodations to an owner of an assistance dog. Fla. Stat. §413.08. Illinois considers a refusal to sell or rent to such a person a violation of civil rights. Ill. Rev. Stat. §3-104.1.

Some states permit disabled people to keep dogs, whether or not the dog is specially trained. The dog owner is responsible for any damage that his pet causes, and a landlord may impose reasonable restrictions in the lease. Cal. Civ. Code §54.1(5).

In addition, a qualified person may not be denied a job merely because his companion is an assistance dog. N.Y. Civ. Rights Law §47a.

The federal government gives special status to some assistance dogs on tax reports. An owner may deduct some of the costs of the dog, including the purchase, training, and maintenance expenses as legitimate medical expenses on his income tax report. Seeing Eye guide dogs are expressly listed in the Federal Tax Regulations. §1.213-1(e)(1)(iii) Income Tax Regulations and Revenue Ruling, volume 1 (1989).

The cost and care of dogs for the blind and the deaf are listed as medical expenses in the government booklet, Federal Tax Regulations §1.214-1(e)(1)(iii) (1989); Publication 17:Chapter 23, page 125 (1988).

If your particular problem is not explicitly stated in the tax laws, write to the chief of your individual tax branch. The office will issue you an opinion letter expressing its conclusion. For further assistance with tax questions, call the Federal Tax Information Hotline at 800-424-1040.

Additionally, the federal government may pay for a guide dog for a veteran entitled to disability compensation. The allowable expenses may include travel and incidental costs to and from home in becoming adjusted to the dog. 38U.S.C. §614.

Under state law, a low-income disabled owner may be entitled to government aid to pay for the expenses of an assistance dog. Both California and New York have a food allowance for guide dogs. N.Y. Soc. Serv. Law §303a; Cal. Welf. & Inst. Code §12553.

Some state courts expressly refuse to allow a creditor to take an assistance dog to satisfy a court judgment against an owner. N.Y. Civ. Prac. Law §5205.

Most states prohibit health aids or personal property from being taken to satisfy a money judgment. An assistance dog should qualify as a health aid or personal property.

If an assistance dog or its owner is injured by another dog, some states double the damage award. In Rhode Island, if the assault occurs a second time, the damage is tripled and the offending dog can be destroyed. R.I. Gen. Laws §4-13-16.1.

Local

Most localities provide an assistance dog with a free license and registration. N.J. Stat. Ann. §4:15.3; Minn. Stat. Ann. §291. A few states issue a permanent license to an assistance dog. Ohio Rev. Code Ann. §955.011.

Most states still require renewal of a license. A special tag will identify the dog as an assistance dog so that it receives the available privileges. The owner is still responsible for the vaccinations.

Most municipalities require a dog license, even for assistance dogs. In many cases the license is free for assistance dogs.

Travel

Assistance dogs experience more travel privileges than other dogs. The law typically allows them to accompany their owners on all types of public transportation, Fla. Stat. §413.08, such as planes, trains, and buses.

Airlines usually have relaxed rules for assistance dogs.

Simply notify the carrier in advance that you will be traveling with an assistance dog. Unlike other dogs, an assistance dog is likely to fly free. The owner will probably be assigned the bulkhead seat, which gives the dog room to sit or lie down at its owner's feet (the dog does not have to fit under the seat). The dog must be properly harnessed, and a health certificate must be attached.

The Delta Society offers for sale a wide variety of resource materials, such as books, journals, slides, video tapes, and audio tapes. The materials discuss pets and the elderly, animal assistance programs, prison programs, therapy programs, as well as many other animal-related topics. For further information, contact:

The Delta Society
P.O. Box 1080
Renton, WA 98057
(206) 226-7357
Fax: (206) 235-1076

DOGS AND THE LAW

Handling a Controversy

A dog can be a nuisance whose
actions can be damaging, even though
the dog is neither vicious nor
threatening.

Handling a Controversy

A dog can be dangerous, or it can be just a nuisance. Either way, if you have a dog like this in your neighborhood, or if you are the owner of the dog, you may have to handle a dispute. Your dog may have caused damage or injury, or it may be the victim. Either way, you must be prepared to manage the encounter in a reasonable, responsible, and legally acceptable manner.

A Dog Attack

A dog attack is an unlikely occurrence; however, it is possible that you may be a victim of, or a witness to, an attack. There are a variety of things you can do to prevent or stop an attack. Most states permit you to take any steps that are reasonably necessary under the circumstances, including killing the dog. Ga. Code Ann. §4-8-5; Ind. Code Ann. §15-5-7-2; R.I. Gen. Laws §4-13-18.

Most dog attacks happen quickly. The event is often over in a matter of seconds because a dog does not remain engaged in battle; it merely bites and releases. Pit bulls, whose instincts and/or training induce a firm hold, may be different.

Get the name and address of the dog and its owner. If that is not possible, write down an accurate description of the dog. This way the dog can be identified at a later time. If the dog is not tagged, the authorities may be able to capture the dog for quarantine. This is to determine if the dog has rabies. If the dog is officially determined to be vicious, it may be destroyed.

Get the names and addresses of all other people, including children, who witnessed the event. Write a short summary of the incident. Memories are short, but a written document lasts a long time.

If a person is injured, get medical attention immediately. A bite or scratch may require medication. A bump or swelling may indicate a sprain or break. All medical bills, including x-rays, therapy, and prescriptions, should be kept as evidence of treatment.

The event should be reported to the local animal control department. This way the dog's ill-tempered nature will be on record. If the dog bites again, it will be on record that the owner had notice of the dog's propensity to cause harm. The dog may already have a history of prior attacks and be considered vicious.

The dog owner should be notified of the incident. Explain to the owner what happened. It may be best to put this in writing which includes a detailed account of the injury and expenses. Assess the damage and negotiate with the owner for a settlement. Ask for a reasonable amount. Often an owner is willing to cover the cost of the injury. Handling the situation directly with the owner is often more expedient than going through insurance companies or the legal system.

Tell the owner that his homeowner's or renter's insurance may cover the event. Many dog owners do not know this. Set a date for payment. Referring to the local law may be persuasive. If an agreement is worked out, put it in writing. This protects you, as well as the owner, if there is a disagreement later on.

If the damage is extensive, or the owner is unwilling to accept responsibility, only then should you consider getting an attorney. Utilizing the legal system can be expensive, time consuming, and nerve wracking. If a lot of money is not involved (less than a few thousand dollars), a less costly alternative is to go to small claims court.

A Nuisance Problem

A dog may not be dangerous, but it can be a nuisance. Some irksome antics include digging up yards, chasing cars, scattering garbage across the lawn, ravaging a prized garden, barking incessantly, roaming the neighborhood, and scaring residents and kids.

If you are the victim, the first thing to do is to talk to the owner. Use a reasonable and friendly approach—avoid animosity. A dog owner will probably be more eager to please a neighbor that does not have a threatening manner. You would be surprised at how many owners do not realize that their dog is disturbing you. Maybe their dog barks only when they are away; or they do not know that their dog is ravaging your garbage cans. A dog owner is usually apologetic and willing to take the necessary steps to control the dog. Maybe you can offer some suggestions as to how to remedy the nuisance, such as keeping the dog indoors after dark, sending it to obedience school, or calling the humane society for advice.

If the dog stops its annoying behavior, take the time to thank the owner. Obviously he took your complaint seriously, so he should know that his corrective measures worked.

If you happen to be the owner of the dog wreaking havoc, be understanding, not hostile. After all, you are responsible for keeping your dog from annoying your neighbors. And your neighbor has probably had several encounters with your dog before he came to talk to you. Take the proper measures to stop the dog's poor behavior. After a few days, visit your neighbor to be sure the problem has been solved.

If talking to your neighbor is a dead-end, try mediation. This method of settling disputes outside of a courtroom involves the imposition of a neutral third party. This individual acts as a link between the disputing parties to keep the lines of communication open. A mediator is not to choose sides, he merely identifies problems and suggests compromises.

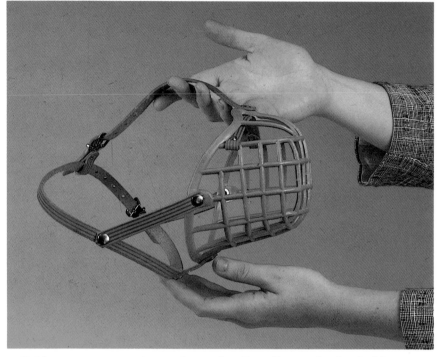

Petshops carry many types of muzzles. Even if your dog is placid, a muzzle on him when he is out in public is highly recommended.

Some communities have professional or volunteer dispute resolution services. Look in the yellow pages, or call your local court house, bar association, chamber of commerce, or police department. Or, a mediator can be a neutral friend or neighbor who is respected by both parties.

Once the differences are settled, define the terms in a writing signed by both parties.

Animal Control Authorities

There may be a reason you do not want to talk to your neighbor, or talking to him was a disaster, or maybe you just do not know who owns the troublesome dog. Call your local police, animal control department, or health/public safety authority. The people responsible for controlling dogs can call or visit the dog owner, or even issue a citation.

These departments may have guidelines to follow. For example, a certain number of complaints may have to be registered before action can be taken. So do not just call and complain. Find out the procedures and follow them up. Look up all the pertinent local law, such as ordinances dealing with noise, vicious dogs, leash laws, nuisances, dogs running at large, personal injury, property damage, or the number of dogs allowed per household, and have it enforced. Enlist the aid of other neighbors who are annoyed. And most importantly, be persistent.

Many communities have professionals or volunteers who are trained in helping you settle minor disputes without going to court or hiring a lawyer. Contact your local authorities , or even the telephone directory, for arbitrators or mediators whose service are usually substantially less expensive than lawyers.

Small Claims Court

An attorney is not needed, and the wait to get before a judge may be as little as a few weeks. Many states have free publications describing the procedures required in their small claims court. A few courts even have advisors to answer questions.

Familiarize yourself with the law so that you can make sure your complaint meets all the required elements. Good preparation is vital to presenting a sound argument. Be brief and articulate, not boring. Present your case in an organized manner. You may be allowed to present witnesses and to utilize documents, police reports, hospital records, medical bills, and photographs. Avoid confusion or repetition. But most importantly, always be respectful to both the judge and your adversary.

Even small claims court imposes some requirements. First, check the jurisdictional limit; small claims court usually restricts the amount to under a few thousand dollars. Second, be sure your complaint is not barred by the statute of limitations; each court has a limited amount of time, as measured from the date of the event, in which you can bring suit. Fortunately, if the annoyance is an on-going event, there is no limit to the number of suits that can be brought. So subsequent events are not barred if a timely suit is commenced.

Third, small claims court restricts your award to money damages; you cannot get an injunction—a court order instructing the dog owner to do or not to do something. However, the number of suits that can be brought is unlimited. Paying damage awards can get expensive and may influence the dog owner to take remedial action.

Fourth, the amount of money recoverable in small claims court may be restricted to actual out-of-pocket expenses; compensation for pain and suffering may be barred.

Attempt to work things out with your neighbor before going to court. Even if not required by law, a judge will probably be more receptive to someone who shows a good faith effort to resolve the dispute out of court.

———

See page 153 for Appendix E, Small Claims Court Jurisditional Limits.

Travel

Rules regarding dog travel are constantly changing from place to place, time to time, and mode of transport. International shipments of dogs are regulated by the carriers (usually airplane companies), the health authorities of both the exporting and importing countries, plus the customs authorities.

Travel

It is a common sight to see a dog owner traveling with his pet. In fact, many owners refuse to go anywhere without their dogs. However, most owners do not realize that traveling is stressful for their pets. So if you are not going to leave your dog at home, at least make the trip as comfortable as possible.

Restrictions regarding pet travel are constantly changing due to health and international situations. Therefore, use this chapter only as a guideline. Always contact the appropriate agricultural department or consulate before departing.

Of course, your dog should be properly identified. The dog's name, and your name, address, and telephone number should be attached to the dog at all times. Most states and countries require a recent certificate of health.

Importing and Exporting

Into the U.S.

The Animal Welfare Act mandates the requirements for importing birds and animals into the U.S. The Department of Agriculture is responsible for setting the standards regarding the transportation, handling, and treatment of dogs. The importing conditions must be humane and healthy.

Each imported container of dogs must be plainly marked, labeled, or tagged on the outside with the names and addresses of the shipper and the consignee. An accurate invoice statement specifying the number of each species contained in the shipment must also be included.

The U.S. Public Health Service stipulates that pets brought into the country be examined at the first port of entry for any evidence of disease communicable to humans. 42 C.F.R. §71.51(b). Since the hours of service and the availability of inspectors vary from port to port, check with your anticipated port of arrival prior to importation. This will reduce the possibility of unnecessary delay.

Dogs are not subject to a mandatory quarantine period (except in Hawaii), nor do they require a health certificate. Dogs are also free of duty.

However, a dog must have a valid rabies vaccination certificate. 42 C.F.R. §71.51(c). The vaccine must have been given at least 30 days prior to entry. The certificate must adequately identify the dog, specify a date of expiration, and bear the signature of a licensed veterinarian. 42 C.F.R. §71.51(a).

Puppies less than six months old which have only been in a rabies-free country (as determined by the Dept. of Health and Human Services), and older dogs living in a rabies-free country for the six months prior to their arrival are excepted. 42 C.F.R. §71.51(c)(1).

A dog failing to meet the rabies vaccination requirement may be admitted if certain criteria are met. The dog must be confined until it is vaccinated, and it must be kept in confinement for at least 30 days after the vaccination date. 42 C.F.R. §71.51(c)(1)(2).

Direct further inquiries to your local customs office or the following agencies:

Dept. of Health and Human Services
Centers for Disease Control
Division of Quarantine
Atlanta, GA 30333
(404) 639-2574

Animal and Plant Health Inspection Service
U.S. Dept. of Agriculture
Hyattsville, MD 20782
(301) 436-7786

Dept. of the Treasury
U.S. Customs Service
Washington, D.C. 20229

Into Foreign Countries

When leaving the U.S., call or write the country into which you want to take your pet, or contact the respective embassy in Washington, D.C., or the nearest consulate office to find out requirements for entry.

Crossing State Boundaries

If you plan to ship your dog by common carrier across state lines, contact the importing state beforehand to learn about regulations regarding crating, inoculations, health certificates, and costs.

The ASPCA publishes booklets concerning pet travel. These include travel tips, interstate travel requirements, and import requirements for the United States, as well as for many foreign countries. For more information and copies contact:

ASPCA Education Department
441 East 92nd Street
New York, NY 10128
(212) 876-7700, ext. 3412

Hawaii

All dogs entering the state of Hawaii are subject to requirements in addition to those already stated for the Department of Health and Human Services. All dogs must complete a 120-day quarantine period at the State Animal Quarantine Station in Oahu.

A dog traveling on an airline must be
contained in a shipping crate. These shipping
crates are usually regulated to insure that the
crate is large enough, secure enough and
properly identifies its contents.

You can ship your dog ahead of your arrival. The airline
will deliver your pet to the Animal Holding Facility. The
State of Hawaii will provide all the necessary transportation.

For additional information, call or write:
State of Hawaii
Dept. of Agriculture
Division of Animal Industry
99-762 Moanalua Road
Aiea, HI 96701-3246
(808) 488-8462

The payment of fees by the owner is due at the time the dog enters quarantine.

You can visit your pet at the facility, or you can designate a friend or relative to watch over your dog. The quarantine station will gladly provide you with a list of groomers and sponsors willing to care for dogs whose owners are not on the island.

Airlines

The Animal Welfare Act protects dogs and other animals traveling on airplanes. This federal regulation requires an airline to refuse to transport an animal unless the following criteria are met: the dog must be 1) at least eight weeks old 9 C.F.R. §3.12(d); 2) certified as healthy within ten days prior to departure; 3) secured in a carrier which meets the standards. 9 C.F.R. §3.12; 4) adequately identified. 9 C.F.R. §3.11.

A dog traveling on an airline must be contained in a shipping crate. The crate must be sturdy and well ventilated. It should be large enough to allow your pet to stand, turn around, and lie down comfortably. The carrier must be marked "Live Animals" and "This End Up." Your name, address, and phone number, the dog's name, and the destination should be on the cage. Cages can be purchased at the airport.

Include a soft, absorbent litter material which is safe and non-toxic to dogs. A favorite toy and an article of clothing with your scent on it make travel more comfortable. Attach a gravity-flow water bottle in such a way that it can be re-filled without having to open the cage. Do not medicate your dog without consulting a veterinarian.

A small–medium size dog can be brought into the cabin as carry-on baggage, or it can be checked into the cargo section. Although the guidelines are similar, each airline has its own restrictions, so call in advance.

Generally, a dog allowed in the cabin as carry-on must be in a carrier small enough fit under the seat. The number of animals permitted on a flight may be limited to one, or it may be determined by the time of year and the type of aircraft. There may also be a restriction as to the number of kennels allowed per passenger. A reservation is required, and there is usually a fee.

Due to the size restriction of carry-on baggage, most dogs must travel in the cargo section. Here there is no size restriction, but all other restrictions apply. The weight of dog and kennel will probably have to be 100 pounds or less. Heavier weights must be checked as air freight. This is more expensive due to the use of the equipment involved to move the cage.

Assistance dogs usually fly for free, and no carrier is necessary. However, guide and hearing dogs must be properly harnessed, and the health certificate must be attached to the harness. The dog does not have to fit under the seat. It must sit or lie at its owner's feet.

There is a chance that your dog may be injured during its journey. The airlines restrict their financial liability to a certain amount regardless of the actual value of your loss. If you want extra coverage, you must declare a higher value for your "baggage" and pay an additional fee. Extra coverage can also be purchased from a private insuror. Since most problems occur on the ground and not during flight time, try to book non-stop flights. Confirm with flight attendants and baggage carriers that your dog is on board.

Cars

Many dogs are accustomed to traveling short distances in a car. However, no pet should be permitted to ride in the front seat, hang out the window, or jump around. A dog must be taught to settle down in the back seat. If your dog is undisciplined, then it must be restrained in a carrier. An uncontrolled dog is a hazard in a moving car.

Periodically allow the dog to exercise and relieve itself. Never leave a dog unattended in the car. It takes only minutes for a car to heat up in the summer and to cool down in the winter. Some states have laws against leaving a dog alone in a car.

Motor Vehicle, Rail, and Marine Carriers

These carriers must also comport to the transportation regulations of the Animal Welfare Act. 9 C.F.R. §3.13. The animal cargo space of these carriers must be designed to protect the health and ensure the safety and comfort of a dog.

Many public transportation vehicles do not allow dogs at all. Some permit dogs if they are secured in a carrier. Assistance dogs, such as guide and hearing dogs, are an exception. Contact the particular bus, train, or boat line to learn its policy. If dogs are allowed, inspect the area if it is separate from where you will be. It should be safe, clean, and well ventilated.

Accommodations

Animalports

At least two airports provide special services for animals. JFK Airport in New York has a facility run by the ASPCA. It services both JFK and LaGuardia terminals. The Animal-Port-Houston is a registered Texas corporation. It has facilities at both the Hobby and Intercontinental airports. These animalports are accessible 24 hours a day, 365 days a year.

A dog can be boarded at an animalport while its owner is away. In addition, the personnel will assist pet owners, shippers, and airlines in handling animals that are being transported. Traveling crates are available for purchase. Dogs traveling alone can spend their layover time at the stress-relieving accommodations. The staff feeds, waters, exercises, and otherwise cares for the residents. Veterinarians are on call. Current vaccinations are required.

A dog may be brought to the JFK Animalport for boarding, or arrangements can be made for pick-up or drop-off

NEVER...BUT NEVER, leave your dog inside a closed car, especially in the summer. Even when it is cool outside, the greenhouse effect of a car's windows could overheat the inside of the car and kill your pet.

service at JFK or LaGuardia airports. For further information, contact:

ASCPA Animalport
JFK International Airport
Air Cargo Building 189
Jamaica, NY 11430
(718) 656-6042
Fax: 718-656-6051
Cable: ANIMALPORT

The Animal-Port-Houston (Texas) will pick up or drop off the dog at your home. Transportation is also available to take your pet anywhere in Houston, such as to the veterinarian, trainer, or groomer. A staff member will even accompany your dog on its flight if you request. Direct further inquiries to:

> Animal-Port-Houston
> P.O. Box 60564 AMF
> Houston, TX 77205
> (713) 821-2244
> FAX: (713) 821-1128

Hotels and Motels

Many hotels and motels do not allow dogs. An exception may or may not be made for an assistance dog. Therefore, it is wise to call in advance or you might find yourself without a place to stay.

Kennels

You may prefer to board your pet. Do not take a chance on just any kennel, though. Your dog deserves reliable accommodations. Inspect any temporary home for your pet. Contact the American Boarding Kennels Association for a reference. They can make a reservation, or they can send you their publication on selecting a kennel.

ABKA   Colorado Springs, CO   (303) 591-1113

Before you board your pet, inspect the kennels for cleanliness, security (against dog escapes and thieves), and costs.

Gaines Pet Foods Corporation publishes a directory of hotels, motels and lodges that permit dogs. Travel tips and coupons for dog products are also included. For your copy, contact:

Gaines TWT
P.O. Box 5700
Kankakee, IL 60902

Dogs Are Property

Dogs Are Property

A dog is personal property. This fact has a lot of legal implications. For instance, since a dog is property, it has no legal rights of its own. A dog can neither sue nor be sued.

An owner of property has legally enforceable rights. The law prohibits a person from injuring, taking, or destroying the property of another. So an owner who has a property interest in his dog is entitled to compensation if his dog is killed, stolen, or injured.

For an owner to enforce his rights as a property owner, though, the dog may need to be licensed. An owner of an unlicensed dog may not be afforded any protection under the law. Often a statute defines only licensed dogs as personal

The law prohibits a person from injuring, taking, or destroying someone else's property. This goes for furniture, as well as another dog..since a dog is property.

Since a dog is property and not people, it cannot be the beneficiary of a will. You can, though, leave the money to a person with instructions to take care of your dog.

property. Ky. Rev. Stat. §258.245; Del Code Ann. §1707. Rights may even be lost if a licensed dog is not wearing its license. Iowa Code Ann. §351.25.

An owner of a puppy, whose young dog does not yet require a license, should still benefit from the property laws concerning dogs. Iowa Code Ann. §351.25.

Damages

A dog owner will probably be able to collect damages from someone who intentionally or negligently kills or injures the dog. If the dog owner is partially responsible for the dog's actions, the damage award may be reduced in relation to the proportion of the owner's fault. Liability will not attach if the dog was killed or injured while attacking a person or livestock, or if the dog was lawfully impounded and destroyed.

83

Damages typically include actual, out-of pocket expenses, such as medical costs. But other criteria may have some bearing as well, including the market value and the age of the dog. *Kearney v. Walker*, 174 Ark. 191, 294 S.W. 407 (1927). Its type, traits, pedigree, and purchase price are all legitimate concerns. *Smith v. Palace Transp. Co.*, 142 Misc. 93, 253 N.Y.S. 87 (1931).

Other considerations include registration, breeding value, value as a watchdog, and if the dog was expecting a litter. *Kling v. U.S. Fire Ins. Co.*, 146 So.2d 635, 1 A.L.R.3d 1011, reh op 146 So.2d 639, 1 A.L.R. 1017 (La.App. 1962). The feelings of the owner may or may not have merit.

Product Liability

A dog may have suffered injury due to a defect in a product. An example may be death from a contaminant in food. A claim such as this is based on product liability. The manufacturer, distributor, wholesaler, or retailer may be held liable on a number of legal theories. First, he may be strictly liable; he is accountable even though there was no fault on his part. Second, he may be held accountable due to negligence; a reasonable person should have foreseen the risk of harm. Third, he may be accountable due to a breach of warranty; the product should have been fit for normal use. Or fourth, he may be liable due to intentional acts; he knew the injuries were substantially certain to result.

Wills

Since a dog is not a person, it cannot be a beneficiary of a will. It cannot inherit money nor other property. If you want your dog to be cared for after your death, you must designate a new owner for the dog in a will. Discuss the provision with the person you intend to be the new owner. Be sure the person which you designate in the will as the new owner really wants the dog, will accept the dog, and is able to care for it.

It is also wise to leave money to the new owner to care for

your dog. Be sure to consider medical expenses, because as your dog gets older its veterinary bills will increase. An alternative is to leave money to the veterinarian. The dollar amount and the services to be rendered should be arranged with the doctor. The will can designate that any money remaining when the dog dies goes to the veterinarian, to another person, or wherever you like.

A court will not enforce a will provision that bequeaths money or property to a dog. Since property cannot inherit property, the dog will not inherit anything. The money or property will be distributed according to the state laws governing succession. Of course, this legal distribution is not likely to be what the person making the will had in mind.

Divorce

A dog may be contested property in a divorce proceeding. A court will determine custody and visitation rights.

Insurance

Your dog may be a pedigreed purebred champion or otherwise unusually valuable. Just like any other property, you can get an insurance policy for your dog. The carrier may reimburse you for the value of the dog. The insurance company will also be the party responsible to bring suit against the person who harmed the dog.

Tax Deduction

No matter how validly a dog is considered a part of the family, the Internal Revenue Service will not permit an owner to list a dog as a dependent. Nor can a dog be claimed as a medical expense, unless it is a guide dog or a hearing dog. Federal Tax Regulations §1.213-1(e)(1)(iii) (1989); Publication 17: "Your Federal Income Tax for Individuals," Chapter 23, page 125 (1988).

For more information, call the Federal Tax Information Hotline at 800-424-1040. Many government publications are available upon request at no charge.

Since dogs are property, they may be contested in divorce proceeding. The court may decide who owns the dog; visitation rights may also be granted.

Taking of Property

Property cannot be taken from an owner without due process of the law. This means that the dog owner must have notice and possibly be given a hearing before his property is taken or destroyed. Therefore, before a dog can be impounded, killed, or offered for adoption, its owner must be given adequate notice. The amount of time considered adequate notice varies from place to place and may depend on whether or not the dog is licensed.

Patents

There is a new trend emerging in the law regarding animal patents. A patent is legal property. In 1988, Harvard University obtained the first patent ever granted for an animal. Since then, the number of pending applications for animal life forms has surged. This patenting of genetic engineering may mean that new dog breeds will be patented. Royalties may have to be paid each time a patented animal gives birth or generates income.

Dog breeds may, in the future, be patentable. Genetic engineering may be a patentable process when used to produce new dog breeds.

DOGS AND THE LAW

General Guidelines for Dog Owners

In most areas, dogs need a
license. Puppies usually are
exempt. A change of ownership
may require a new license. A
change of domicile may also
require a new license, especially
if it's in another state. In many
areas unlicensed dogs may be
impounded.

General Guidelines
for Dog Owners

Licenses

Probably wherever you live, a dog needs a license. A license involves a fee. It usually has to be renewed periodically. It should be worn by the dog at all times. Iowa Code Ann. §351.8. In most areas, a dog license can be gotten by mail.

A license may be valid throughout the entire state. Some licenses, though, are good only in the city or county that issued them. If you move to another state, your dog will almost surely need a new license. If the dog gets a new owner, the old license may be transferable, or a new license may be required.

Puppies under a certain age are exempt from licensing requirements. A license may cost less for a spayed or neutered dog, an assistance dog, or a dog belonging to an elderly or disabled person. A special license may be in order if you breed, sell, or keep more than a certain number of dogs.

To find out where to get a license, talk to your pet shop owner, veterinarian, city or county officials, the animal control or health department, or look in the telephone book.

Licensed and unlicensed dogs may be accorded different treatment under the law. You may not be able to take advantage of property rights if your dog is unlicensed. Some statutes state that property laws apply only to licensed dogs. Ky. Rev. Stat. §258.245; Del. Code Ann. §1707.

Any unlicensed dog, Ann. Ind. Code §15-5-9-14, or an unlicensed dog running at large, N.J. Stat. Ann. §4:15.16, may be impounded, then destroyed or offered for adoption. Unlicensed dogs that are impounded are killed or sold sooner than licensed dogs, because local authorities are unable to trace ownership. Furthermore, some states permit the killing of an unlicensed dog, Del. Code Ann. §1708, or a licensed dog not wearing its license, Iowa Code Ann. §351.26, at any time. Yet a dog wearing a license can be killed only if it is attacking a person or livestock. Iowa Code Ann. §351.27.

If your dog is lost or stolen, it will be harder to find if it does not have a license. An owner of an unlicensed dog may be subject to a fine or penalty.

Vaccinations

A current rabies vaccination is a common requirement in most locales. Many states require a dog to get a rabies vaccination in order to get a license. A free anti-rabies clinic may be offered periodically. D.C. Code §6-1003(b). Other injections, such as a distemper shot, may be required as well. D.C. Code §6-1003(a).

Often a veterinarian administering shots must issue a report to the local authorities. This is one way that the government makes sure that owners register their dogs. Puppies under a certain age are not required to be vaccinated. Proof of current vaccinations may be necessary before you can transport your dog to another state or country.

Spaying and Neutering

Some states have established clinics where dogs can be spayed or neutered. Conn. Gen. Stat. Ann. §22-380a. Some communities offer free sterilization services on a periodic basis. A license may cost less for a spayed or neutered dog than for one which has not been altered. Ann. Ind. Code §15-5-9-1.

Leash Laws

Many jurisdictions have leash laws. These laws require a dog to be under the control of its owner at all times. This may involve confinement, that the dog be on a leash, or even muzzled. No dog should be allowed to roam free. A dog at large could be impounded and disposed of according to the regulation. Del. Code Ann. §1712. Its owner may be fined and have to pay for the cost of confining the dog. Some communities have areas where dogs are allowed to run loose.

Vehicles

A dog should never be left alone in a car. It takes only a few minutes for the heat to become unbearable in the summer, and to drop to freezing in the winter. Some towns actually prohibit a dog from being left alone in a car. An owner may be violating anti-cruelty laws.

A dog traveling in a car or truck should be well-behaved. An undisciplined dog can be deadly in a moving vehicle. The dog should be trained to lie in the back seat of a car. Allowing your dog to stick its head out of the window is unwise. The dog may jump, or it may get something in its eye. Some manufacturers sell seat belts and car seats designed for dogs.

A dog may be prohibited from riding in the back of a vehicle unless it is enclosed or has side and tail racks of a certain height. The vehicle should have a means of preventing the dog from being thrown out. A dog may have to be caged or cross-tethered in the open bed of a pick-up truck. Cal. Veh. Code §23117.

Other Restrictions

Muzzle laws are becoming more popular, as are laws requiring owners to clean up their dog's solid waste (pooper-scooper laws) if it is deposited anywhere off their own property. Many buildings, such as restaurants, apartments, and hotels, and other areas, such as beaches, Del. Code Ann. §1715, are strictly off limits to dogs. Owners of assistance dogs are commonly excluded from these laws.

Many areas have leash laws which require that a dog be under the direct, positive control of its master at all times. When the dog is being walked it must be on a leash. Most petshops carry a large assortment of collars and leashes which consider the dog's size and the length of the leash that you need.

How Many Dogs Allowed?

Many animal lovers have more than one dog. However, some communities restrict the number of dogs allowed per household, and some residences refuse to permit dogs at all.

These laws are taken quite seriously. If your condominium or apartment lease has a no-pets clause, you can be evicted for harboring a dog. If your residence limits the number of dogs you can keep, exceeding that number can subject you to a daily fine.

Some communities restrict the number of dogs per household. If you want to keep more pets, you may need to apply for a city permit or a kennel license. This may entail extra fees, rules, and inspections.

**Lost dogs which have no dog tags or
license may be impounded, sold,
destroyed, or given out for adoption.**

Some cities may require multiple-dog owners to obtain a kennel license. A kennel license is more expensive than a regular dog license. Your premises may need to meet certain requirements and be subject to inspection by the authorities.

The law may make an exception for puppies or dogs kept only temporarily. However, there may be no exceptions. Familiarize yourself with the law before breeding a dog. This saves you a lot of frustration in the future.

An owner may be required to dispose of the number of dogs exceeding the allowable limit. Fines and jail sentences can be imposed as well. These enforcement measures can be imposed even if you are caring for someone else's dog temporarily. Puppies under a certain age may or may not be excepted.

Lost and Found

If your dog is lost, call any agency that you think handles dogs. Include the police, health and animal control departments, and humane societies. Listen to local radio stations and read the local newspapers that list found animals. Visit the police station, animal shelter and city hall—wherever lists may be posted. Some agencies refuse to give out information over the phone. Leave a picture and an accurate description of the dog in every place you visit. If at first you are not successful, keep asking around. The dog may show up later.

If you find a dog, attempt to find its owner, or give the dog to the local authorities. If you do not make an effort to return the dog to its owner, you may be liable to the owner for the value of the dog. Some states require you to call the animal control authorities. If the law requires you to turn the dog in to a shelter, ask to have the first chance at adoption.

A pound with custody of the dog is responsible for finding the owner. It probably has a procedure for making a public announcement if the dog is not tagged.

If the dog remains in your possession, check for identification. The dog may have the name and address of its owner on a tag. Call the owner. If the dog has a license tag, call the agency that issued the tag to get the name of the owner. Ask local residents if they recognize the dog. Post signs around the area where the dog was found. Put a notice in the paper and notify the local radio station.

Impoundment

Laws often give animal control officials the authority to pick up, impound, sell, and destroy dogs. However, since a dog is considered the personal property of its owner, a dog cannot be confiscated without notice, and possibly a hearing.

An owner's property rights may be lost, however, only under certain conditions. Any unlicensed dog, Ann. Ind. Code §15-5-9-14, a dog running at large without a vaccination tag, Iowa Code Ann. §351.37, or running at large without a license tag, Iowa Code Ann. §351.25, may be impounded without first notifying its owner.

Dogs running around loose are typical pound inhabitants. Injured, abandoned, and vicious dogs also end up at the pound. A dog that has bitten a person, caused damage, or been declared a nuisance can be taken from its owner and impounded. An owner who has his dog in his possession, though, is entitled to be notified before the dog is seized. An owner must be notified again before the dog is destroyed. Most states even give the owner a chance in court to argue that the dog should not be killed.

A pound is required to keep the dog for a prescribed period of time before it can take action. The holding time can vary anywhere from one to 14 days. If the owner can be identified, he must be notified. To reclaim the dog, an owner may have to have the dog licensed and vaccinated, pay a fine, and pay a charge for every day the dog was kept. If the owner does not claim the dog, it can be sold, offered for adoption, or killed in a humane manner.

The law may allow a dog to be donated to an assistance dog agency. Ohio Rev. Code Ann. §955.16(A)(3). Some states declare it unlawful to knowingly sell or give away an impounded dog for experimentation. Hawaii Rev. Stat. §143-

18. Other states may permit a dog to be sold to a research or teaching facility. That facility may have to be certified by the state. Ohio Rev. Code Ann. §955.16(B). A pound that turns dogs over for research may have to post a sign stating as much. Cal. Civ. Code §1834.7. A pound can make a new owner have the dog spayed or neutered. The adoption fee may include the price of required vaccinations.

> A dog pound is usually required to keep a stray dog for a period of one to 14 days before it disposes of the animal. It must use its best effort to locate the owner if the dog is licensed and is wearing its identification tag. If the dog remains unclaimed, the pound can sell it, offer it for adoption, or kill it in a humane manner.

Dogs are controlled for many reasons. They carry fleas and ticks and may spread diseases such as rabies.

Animal Control Authorities

Dog laws may be enforced by any number of agencies. These include the police, a humane society, an animal control center or a health department. No matter which organization is responsible for enforcing the law, it must respect the legal rights of an owner. If your dog is wrongfully impounded and is sold, destroyed, suffers some injury, or becomes ill as a result, you may be able to sue. You must be able to prove that you did not receive the proper notice, that the animal was improperly taken, or that it was kept after you tried to get it out. If the authorities did not violate any of their procedures about notice and confinement, your chances of winning are minimal.

Insurance

If you have a dangerous or vicious dog, you may be required by statute to have liability insurance. The policy should pay for any damage or injury done by your dog, as well as any injury sustained by your pet. It is wise to have liability coverage for every dog. Given the right circumstances, any dog can cause harm.

You may want to get a health insurance policy for your dog. This insurance will pay for medical expenses, including veterinarian bills, hospital fees and medications. Medical attention required for sickly or older dogs can be quite expensive. Some states limit the types of insurance firms that can offer pet health insurance. N.J. Stat. Ann. §17:46-D).

Burial

Contact your local animal control authority for information on how to dispose of your dog's remains. Although many dog owners bury their pet in their own yard, many towns have ordinances against this. The carcass cannot be left on public property unless the area is a public dump or other such facility. Ga. Code Ann. §4-8-2.

The dog may have to be brought to a cemetery. The wisest thing to do is to have your vet handle the burial. Some towns will dispose of the dog for a fee.

Many owners think of their dogs as family members. Therefore, losing a pet can induce intense grief. Often friends and family members do not share the same depth of loss, though.

Bide-a-Wee provides free counseling for bereaved pet owners. Information on how to cope with pet loss and bereavement is available from:

Delta Society
P.O. Box 1080
Renton, WA 98057
(206) 226-7357
Fax: (206) 235-1076

Proposed Changes to the Animal Welfare Act

Proposed Changes to the Animal Welfare Act

The Animal Welfare Act regulates the handling, treatment, and care of animals. Proposed revisions and amendments to 9 CFR, parts 1, 2, and 3, have been published in the Federal Register/Vol. 54, No. 49/Wednesday, March 15, 1989. These federal proposals concern dealers, exhibitors, research facilities, and transporters. Private owners are not affected. These

The Animal Welfare Act affects commercial aspects of dog handling, like petshops, dealers (breeders), exhibitors, researchers, and transporters. It probably also may affect kennels and veterinarians. It does not affect how nice you are to your family pet.

Enclosures must allow the dog to stand up. The minimum height must be six inches above the head of a standing dog contained within the enclosure...or a fence six feet high must restrain a tethered dog.

rules are important because, if accepted, they are likely to be incorporated into state and local ordinances. Some of the revisions are summarized below.

Humidity 9 CFR §3.2(b)

Indoor facilities housing dogs will have a new humidity standard. The humidity must be maintained between 30 and 70 percent.

Enclosures 9 CFR §3.6

Enclosures for dogs will have a height requirement. The minimum height must be at least six inches above the highest point on the tallest dog, when it is standing, in the enclosure. A fence at least six feet high must confine chained or tethered dogs.

Exercise and Socialization 9 CFR §3.7

A dog should be able to see and hear other dogs. If only one dog is kept at a facility, the animal must receive positive, physical human contact at least 60 minutes per day.

Dogs kept in cages less than four times the required floor space, and that do not have contact with other dogs, must be allowed to exercise and socialize every day for at least 30 minutes.

Transport 9 CFR §3.13, 3.14

A dog ready for transport must have a certificate specifying the date and time it last received food and water. The amount of time the dog could be held at a terminal waiting to be picked up would be limited.

Transport containers would need to have ventilation in each of their four walls. The openings must be at least eight percent of the total surface of each wall.

Puppies less than 180 days old may not be transported in the same enclosure with an adult dog other than its dam. When shipped by air, no more than two live dogs, older than eight weeks, comparable in size, and over 20 pounds each, may be transported in the same enclosure. For puppies under 20 pounds each, three may be shipped per container. When shipped by land, a maximum of four dogs may be transported in the same enclosure.

Additional Requirements for Research Facilities 9 CFR §2.30

Research facilities must ensure that adequate veterinary care, including the appropriate use of drugs or euthanasia, is provided at all times. Pain and distress must be minimized. The attending veterinarian has the authority to inspect all animal areas at any time.

When performing procedures that might reasonably be expected to be painful, the research facility must give assurance that alternative procedures were considered, but were not suitable. The chosen experiment must not unnecessarily duplicate previous experiments. Pain relieving drugs, anesthetics, analgesics, and tranquilizers must be used to minimize pain.

Buying and Selling

Buying and Selling

Pet Shop

Most of the laws regulating buyers, sellers and breeders of dogs pertain to dealers. A dealer is a person who buys and sells dogs in the regular course of his business. The definition of a dealer may include breeders, pet shops, and brokers. An owner who sells the family pet's puppies at a yard sale is not covered. However, some laws do encompass the occasional seller. The law may deal more strictly with someone engaged in business, but an individual still has responsibility as well.

If you regularly sell, keep, or breed more than a certain number of dogs, you may need a kennel or breeder's license. Puppies may or may not be included in this number. Usually diseased dogs and dogs under a specified age (usually eight weeks) cannot be sold.

Whether you are the buyer or the seller, put the sales agreement in writing. Until you write it out, you may not realize that you and the other party have different understandings. Both parties should sign the certificate. The agreement should include, but is certainly not limited to, the following disclosures:

1. The breed, sex, age, color, quality, and birth date.
2. The names and addresses of the buyer and the seller.

Petshops are regulated by laws. These laws vary from one place to another. The laws protect you and in almost all cases allow you to return the dog for a full refund if the dog becomes unhealthy or undesirable. If you buy your pet from a local breeder, you may not have this protection, which is one good reason why you should buy your dog from a petshop.

107

3. The name and address of the breeder.

4. The name and address of the party from whom the dog was purchased.

5. The names and registration numbers of the sire and dam (pedigree).

6. Litter number.

7. The name and registration number of the dog.

8. The date the dealer took possession.

9. The date shipped to the dealer.

10. The date of veterinary exams, the name and address of the veterinarian, and any findings and treatments.

11. The date and types of vaccinations.

12. The behavior (viciousness) and propensities (training) of the dog.

13. Any health problems the dog may have.

14. Any warranties (guarantees) the seller is making.

15. Price.

Additional requirements may regulate the sale and breeding of vicious dogs. A seller may have to notify local animal authoritites if he sells a dog that he knows to be dangerous. Ohio Rev. Code Ann. §955.11(D).

A dissatisfied buyer has a limited period of time, typically 14 days, in which he can return the dog. Within that time, the buyer should be able to return the dog for a refund, or to exchange it for another dog of equivalent value. In some instances, the buyer may be able to keep the dog and recover the difference between the actual value paid and the actual value of the dog received. Cal. Civ. Code §3343(a).

The buyer may also be able to bill the seller for veterinary costs. Some states allow a purchaser several days to return a dog after a veterinarian has certified that the animal is unfit. Va. Code Ann. §3.1-796.80.

Pet Shops

Anyone who wants to operate as a dealer must obtain a license. 9 CFR §2.1 Compliance with standards for facilities, 9 CFR §2.3, and record keeping requirements, 9 CFR §2.75, as set forth in the Animal Welfare Act, must be maintained.

Typically, pet stores must have a veterinarian examine puppies prior to being offered for sale, and at reasonable intervals until sold. The pet shop must ensure appropriate health care. Usually sick animals, and those who have not been examined by a veterinarian, must be quarantined.

Cages, bowls, food bins, utensils, floors and counter tops should be cleaned and disinfected regularly. Fecal material should be removed daily. Wire floors or grates lessen the chance of spreading disease. Food should be stored in covered containers. Food must be replaced daily. The water should be clean and fresh. A pet shop that does not provide adequate care may be committing a misdemeanor. Va. Code Ann. §3.1-796.71.

Some states impose cage labeling requirements. The tag may have to include the supplier's name and address, the sex and breed of the dog, its place and date of birth, the name of its veterinarian, and dates of examination.

Typically, a purchaser has 14 days in which to return a dog suffering from an illness or other condition, at the time of the sale, which adversely affects its health. The dog can be exchanged for one of similar value, or the consumer can get a refund for the price of the dog. The law may allow the pet owner to retain the dog. Reimbursement of veterinary fees, up to a certain amount, to certify the dog unfit or to cure it may be recovered. A purchaser may have no legal recourse if he mistreats or neglects the dog.

Some states require pet stores to provide customers with a statement of consumer rights and remedies and to post a notice. The dealer may be legally obligated to explain the notice orally. The consumer may have to sign a form certifying that he understands his options. Either the dealer or the consumer can initiate legal action.

The purchaser may have to notify the seller of problems within a limited amount of time after receiving veterinary certification. It may be necessary to provide the seller with the telephone number of the doctor.

Landlords understandably prefer not to rent to dog owners. Many landlords can legally charge additional rent to a dog owner. Dogs are, by nature, diggers. They cover their excrement, bury bones and search for hidden "treasures." Check your lease to see if you have a NO PET clause before you buy a dog; many landlords will negotiate a no pet clause.

Landlords, Tenants, and Dogs

Landlords, Tenants, and Dogs

Many landlords prefer not to rent to dog owners. A dog can disturb other tenants if it is noisy, messy, or smelly. Under the right circumstances, any dog can destroy property or injure a person. The dog can cause the landlord a lot of aggravation and expense. A landlord who knew of a dog's poor behavior and could have controlled or removed it, but did nothing, could be legally liable for the dog's antics.

Violation of an existing no-pets clause may be a sufficient cause for eviction or a penalty. Some condominiums or apartments forbid or limit the number of dogs that can be kept. An exception may or may not be made for puppies or dogs kept only temporarily.

A no-dogs policy may be negotiable. An exception may be made if the prospective tenant can assure the landlord that the dog will not be a problem. But how do you convince the landlord?

There are several things that can be done. Introduce the dog to the landlord. The landlord can see for himself that the dog is well groomed and well mannered. An untrained puppy is not as desirable as a mature adult dog. A spayed or neutered dog will probably get bonus points. Bring along written references from previous landlords and neighbors saying that the dog has not been a problem and is well liked.

Special provisions can be negotiated in private leases that are fair to both sides. A higher rent and a substantial damage deposit may be required. The landlord can define the types of damage and repairs that must be paid by the tenant, both while the tenant lives in the apartment and after he moves out. The lease can limit the number, type, and size of a tenant's dog. Liability insurance may be necessary. The tenant may be required to clean up the dog's droppings from the yard. The dog may have to remain inside during certain hours.

A landlord is permitted to demand that a dog owner take reasonable precautions to control the dog. This is because a landlord who has knowledge that a tenant has a vicious dog, but fails to take adequate measures to prevent harm, may be liable for any damage done by the dog. *Strunk v. Zoltanski*, 62 N.Y.2d 572, 468 N.E.2d 13, 479 N.Y.S.2d 175 (1984).

A rental agreement is a contract that is enforceable for a specific period of time. Its provisions can only be changed by the agreement of both the tenant and the landlord. It cannot be altered unilaterally. Either party is free to renegotiate the terms of the rental contract when it comes up for renewal.

To prevent a landlord from inserting a no-pets clause as an excuse for evicting a tenant with a dog, some states require that any changes in the lease be reasonable. If the dog is a nuisance, the tenant must be given an opportunity to correct the problem before commencement of eviction proceedings. If the dog is not a nuisance, the tenant may argue that the no-pets clause is unreasonable.

A lease may contain a no-pets clause. However, if that clause has not been enforced for a long time, the landlord may have lost his right to object. A landlord may have only a specific period of time to enforce a no-pets clause after finding out about a tenant's pet. The tenant may argue that the no-pets clause is being enforced arbitrarily.

Tenants in public housing are not usually allowed to have dogs. Owners of assistance dogs, though, cannot be denied housing merely because they have a companion dog.

Federal laws also permit the elderly and the disabled to have a dog, even if the dog is not specially trained. Landlords can include reasonable provisions in the lease. Dog owners are still responsible for damage and injury caused by their dogs.

There are many pooper-scooper laws which require the dog owner to clean up after a dog has deposited solid waste, overturned a garbage can or otherwise messed up an area. Any thoughtful dog owner would naturally clean up after his or her dog made a mess.

Veterinarians

Veterinarians

Your dog is probably like a member of your family, so find a veterinarian you trust. You should feel comfortable with the doctor because you will be relying on his professional judgment when it comes to caring for your dog.

A veterinarian should take the time to explain diagnoses, treatments, and costs. If you do not understand, ask questions. Get the specifics in writing, if the treatment and costs are extensive. This will avoid unpleasantness in the future. Your dog's medical expenses cannot be deducted from your income tax. However, you can purchase health insurance for your pet. You might want to arrange a lifetime care contract with the veterinarian. The idea is to have the doctor provide medical services for your dog, in exchange for a lump sum, from the time of your death until the dog's death.

A veterinarian can euthanise a sick or older dog at your request. He can also dispose of the dog's remains. A healthy dog probably will not be put to sleep on demand. The veterinarian is likely to suggest alternatives or will try to find a new owner.

A veterinarian is not responsible for a dog indefinitely. A dog that is not retrieved by its owner from the veterinarian's office after a specified amount of time, usually 14 days, is considered abandoned. The doctor should attempt to find a new owner. If a new owner cannot be found, the dog can be destroyed. Cal. Civ. Code §1834.5; Va. Code Ann. §3.1-796.75. The dog must be destroyed in a humane manner. Ga. Code Ann. §4-8-5(b).

If a veterinarian cannot locate the owner of a sick or injured dog, the doctor can treat, hospitalize, or euthanize the dog without the prior permission of the owner. No liability will attach. Va. Code Ann. §3.1-796.76.

A veterinarian or a staff member may be injured by a dog during the course of its treatment. The dog owner is probably not responsible because the veterinarian and his assistants know and accept the risk of injury. A court may also consider that a doctor's treatment provoked a dog to bite. A doctor has insurance to cover these mishaps. Of course, an owner cannot conceal the fact that his dog is dangerous.

If you are unsure or dissatisfied with the veterinarian's recommendations, discuss it with the family doctor. Get a second medical opinion. If a dispute arises, bring in a disinterested third party to mediate. You can lodge a complaint with the state licensing agency or the local veterinary association. The matter can be investigated and disciplinary action taken.

Go to court only as a last resort. Proving that malpractice (legal incompetence or carelessness) caused an injury is difficult. Translating the death or injury of a dog into a dollar amount may also be difficult. The cost of a legal battle is likely to be more than the recoverable damages. If a dog died at the doctor's office, the veterinarian may have the burden of proving that malpractice was not a factor.

Once a dog has bitten a person, or exhibited menacing behavior, it may be officially designated a vicious dog. This definition may apply to your toy poodle who barks or bites the mailman. Some dogs, however, like pit bull terriers, have been bred for generations to be fighters. You may be obligated to protect the public from exposure to such an animal.

Vicious Dogs
and Pit Bulls

This lovely drawing by Misao
Fishwick shows a fantasy of pit bulls
and dog fights. It was used to
illustrate the classic book on dog
fighting, BLAZER, THE STORY OF A
FIGHTING DOG, by Nicholas Forster
(ISBN 0-86622-547-1).

Vicious Dogs and Pit Bulls

Once a dog has bitten a person or exhibited menacing behavior, it may be officially declared a vicious dog. An unlicensed dog, one that engages in dog fighting, or one that has been trained to make unprovoked attacks may be considered vicious. Police dogs are usually exempt from the standard definition of a dangerous dog. Ohio Rev. Code Ann. §955.11.

Usually a hearing is held to determine if a dog is vicious. However, a few kinds of dog breeds are believed to be inherently dangerous. One such dog is the pit bull. This creates a legal problem, though, because there is no such breed of dog known simply as the pit bull. The name describes a group of dogs, including bulldogs, terriers, and mixed breeds containing an element of such breeds. These dogs have been bred and trained to be strong and aggressive.

Read the law carefully. It should clearly establish which dogs are considered pit bulls. If the law is not specific enough, it may be unconstitutional due to vagueness. Dog owners have to be given fair warning.

Some animal lovers are opposed to dog laws that are breed specific. They consider a law that singles out pit bulls as arbitrary because all types of dog breeds can be vicious. However, animal rights enthusiasts will usually support legislation that governs all dangerous dogs.

Responsibility of Owners

Owners of such vicious dogs may be required to take strict measures to control their dogs. A vicious dog may have to be securely confined indoors or enclosed in a locked kennel or pen. When the dog is in any public place or common area (such as the hallway of an apartment building), it must be leashed and muzzled. If the dog is in a motor vehicle, the vehicle must be locked and have a closed roof.

Obtaining a potentially dangerous dog license may be a

mandatory procedure. The dog may receive a registration number and a special identification tag. The registration number may have to be tattooed on the dog. A photograph of the dog may be kept on file. The dog may have to be spayed or neutered at the owner's expense. Owning or harboring a vicious animal may be considered a nuisance. R.I. Gen. Laws Ann. §4-13.1-1(d).

The law may bar a person younger than 18 years old from owning a vicious dog. The owner may be required to have liability insurance for the dog. Signs may be necessary to warn the public that a vicious dog is on the premises. Such a sign may have to contain a symbol designed to inform children that a dangerous dog is present. Ga. Code Ann. §4-8-25(b)(2).

A bond may have to be posted with the municipality to cover any potential injury or damage. Some cities totally ban vicious dogs. In the event that a dog known to be vicious is sold, Ohio Rev. Code Ann. §955.11(D), lost, stolen, dies, is running loose, or attacks a human, Ga. Code Ann. §4-8-25(d), the owner may have to notify the proper authorities.

A person who owns or keeps a vicious dog may be guilty of a misdemeanor or a felony. Alabama Code §3-1-29.

An owner who fails to comply with the law may be fined or imprisoned. Ga. Code Ann. §4-8-28. He may also be liable for double or triple the amount of damage caused by the dog. A vicious dog that is considered a serious danger may be impounded and killed. Its owner is entitled to a notice and a hearing.

A California court held that the owner of a pit bull that mauled a two-year-old toddler to death could be tried on a charge of second-degree murder. The court was unmoved by the owner's claims that the dog was chained and had never bitten a human before. The dog had been bred to fight and was trained to serve as an attack dog. The court said the evidence supported the inference that the owner may have been aware that the dog was potentially dangerous to humans. *Berry v. Superior Court*, No. 117825, March, 1989.

Using dogs for scientific research is usually not punishable by law. The use of dogs for toxicity and effectiveness studies of human drugs is extensive and well documented. Many Humane groups protest the use of dogs as experimental animals; yet Humane Societies put thousands of dogs to death every year because they are strays or otherwise undesirable. The courts have been called upon to evaluate these extreme positions.

Cruelty

Cruelty against dogs is forbidden.

Cruelty

Cruelty against dogs is forbidden. Inhumane treatment may include intentional abuse, neglect, theft, abandonment, and dog fighting. Cropping ears and tails without using anesthesia, leaving a dog which was hit by your car, confining a dog in a parked car, and poor conditions in a pet shop, may all be considered cruelty. It is lawful, though, to kill a dog in the act of injuring a person or damaging property. In the United Kingdom, all ear cropping is prohibited.

If you suspect improper behavior, first talk to the owner. If the maltreatment does not cease, report the abuse to the humane society, the police, a local dog society, and anyone else you think has the right to take action. It is best to have the complaint in writing. Keep a copy for yourself.

Except in the case of an emergency, the dog owner is entitled to notice before the dog can be taken away. A mistreated dog can be seized by the authorities and impounded. If the cruelty is particularly outrageous, the abuser may be subject to a fine or a jail sentence. The owner may also have to pay for the cost of impoundment before he can get the dog back.

A dog may have to be killed by a veterinarian, a pound, or a dealer. The dog must be destroyed in a manner that causes as little pain as possible.

Research

Using dogs for scientific research is usually not punishable by law. The experimentation has practical medical benefits, such as advancing the study of cancer, diabetes, alcoholism, heart disease, infectious diseases, drugs, and surgical treatments. The number of dogs and other animals used for scientific research is estimated to be in the millions. Millions of unclaimed dogs, though, are also killed each year by animal shelters.

There are about 7,000 animal rights groups in the United States. They question the moral justification for sacrificing animals for the benefit of mankind. Their demands range from securing better lab conditions to setting all the animals free.

The troubling conditions at respected research centers have improved over the years. The number of animals used in experimentation has declined as other research methods have been developed. The conditions of care in the research facilities have changed for the better.

Each research facility must obtain a federal registration. 9 CFR §2.25. It must conform to the standards 9 CFR §2.26, and record keeping requirements, 9 CFR §2.76, of the Animal Welfare Act. Proposed amendments to the Act require improved laboratory conditions. The changes call for a reduction in the number of animals sacrificed, the refinement of techniques that cause suffering, and the replacement of live animals with simulations or cell cultures where possible. A national data bank will list the results of all animal experiments so that repetition will be minimized. Laboratories must set up animal-care committees, submit to regular inspections, provide larger cages, and allow the animals to exercise and socialize regularly.

Some institutions have implemented their own reforms without waiting for legal compulsion. They keep the animals mentally and emotionally stimulated by providing games and activities. Some firms have pledged to halt animal tests as soon as alternatives are available. A few cosmetics companies have discontinued using animals in their product testing.

The moral debate rages on. Some scientists consider the reforms excessive. Animal rights activists claim that the reforms are too modest.

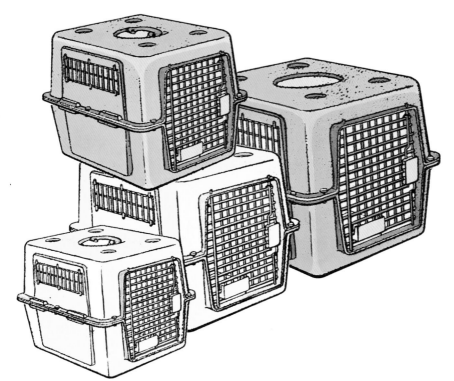

Petshops have many sizes of carrying kennels which are easily cleaned, well ventilated and sturdy. These carrying kennels can be used for transporting your dog, training or restraining him.

Your pet dog can be a nuisance to your neighbors if he barks or howls incessantly, or even intermittently. As a good neighbor, control your dog. If you love your dog yet cannot control his howling, your veterinarian may suggest an operation to remove the dog's voice box. This is a good alternative to having the dog destroyed.

Appendices

127

Appendix A

State Code Books

Abbreviation	*Full Title*
Ala. Code	Code of Alabama
Alaska Stat.	Alaska Statutes
Ann. Mis. Stat.	Annotated Missouri Statutes
Ariz. Rev. Stat. Ann.	Arizona Revised Statutes Annotated
Ark. Stat. Ann.	Arkansas Statutes Annotated
Cal. (subject) Code	Annotated California Code
Colo. Rev. Stat. Ann.	Colorado Revised Statutes Annotated
Conn. Gen. Stat.	General Statutes of Connecticut
Conn. Gen. Stat. Ann.	Connecticut General Statutes Annotated
Cons. Law of N.Y.	Consolidated Law of N.Y.
D.C. Code Ann.	District of Columbia Code Annotated
D.C. Code Encycl.	District of Columbia Code Encyclopedia
Del. Code Ann.	Delaware Code Annotated
Fla. Stat.	Florida Statutes
Fla. Stat. Ann.	Florida Statutes Annotated
Ga. Code Ann.	Code of Georgia Annotated
Hawaii Rev. Stat.	Hawaii Revised Statutes
Idaho Code	Idaho Code
Ill. Rev. Stat.	Illinois Revised Statutes
Ill. Ann. Stat.	Illinois Annotated Statutes
Ind. Code	Indiana Code
Ind. Code Ann.	Annotated Indiana Code or Indiana Statutes Annotated Code
Iowa Code	Code of Iowa
Iowa Code Ann.	Iowa Code Annotated
Kan. Stat. Ann.	Kansas Statutes Annotated
Ky. Rev. Stat.	Kentucky Revised Statutes
Ky. Rev. Stat. Ann.	Kentucky Revised Statutes Annotated
La. Rev. Stat. Ann.	Louisiana Revised Statutes Annotated

La. Civ. Code Ann.	Louisiana Civil Code Annotated
L.S.A.	Louisiana Civil Code
Mass. Gen. Laws Ann.	Massachusetts General Laws Annotated
Mass. Ann. Laws	Annotated Laws of Massachusetts
Md. (subject) Code Ann.	Annotated Code of Maryland
Md. Ann. Code	Maryland Annotated Code
Me. Rev. Stat. Ann.	Maine Revised Statutes Annotated
Mich. Comp. Laws	Michigan Compiled Laws
Mich. Comp. Laws Ann.	Michigan Compiled Laws Annotated
Mich. Stat. Ann.	Michigan Statutes Annotated
Minn. Stat.	Minnesota Statutes
Minn. Stat. Ann.	Minnesota Statutes Annotated
Miss. Code	Mississippi Code
Miss. Code Ann.	Mississippi Code Annotated
Mo. Ann. Stat.	Annotated Missouri Statutes
Mont. Code Ann.	Montana Code Annotated
Mo. Rev. Stat.	Missouri Revised Statutes
N.C. Gen. Stat. Ann.	General Statutes of North Carolina Annotated
N.D. Cent. Code Ann.	North Dakota Century Code Annotated
Neb. Rev. Stat.	Revised Statutes of Nebraska
Nev. Rev. Stat. Ann.	Nevada Revised Statutes Annotated
N.H. Rev. Stat. Ann.	New Hampshire Revised Statutes Annotated
N.J.S.A.	New Jersey Statutes Annotated
N.J. Stat. Ann.	New Jersey Statutes Annotated
N.M. Stat. Ann.	New Mexico Statutes Annotated
N.Y. (subject) Law	Consolidated Laws of New York Annotated
Ohio Rev. Code Ann.	Ohio Revised Code Annotated
Okla. Stat.	Oklahoma Statutes
Okla. Stat. Ann.	Oklahoma Statutes Annotated
Ore. Rev. Stat.	Oregon Revised Statutes
Pa. Cons. Stat.	Pennsylvania Consolidated Statutes
Pa. Cons. Stat. Ann.	Pennsylvania Consolidated Statutes Annotated

Pa. Stat. Ann.	Pennsylvania Statutes Annotated
P.R. Laws Ann.	Puerto Rico Laws Annotated
R.I. Gen. Laws Ann.	General Laws of Rhode Island Annotated
S.C. Code Ann.	Code of Laws of South Carolina Annotated
S.D. Codified Laws Ann.	South Dakota Codified Laws Annotated
S.D. Comp. Laws Ann.	South Dakota Compiled Laws Annotated
South Dak. Codif. Laws	South Dakota Codified Laws
Tenn. Code Ann.	Tennessee Code Annotated
Tex. (subject) Code Ann.	Texas Codes Annotated
Tex. Stat. Ann.	Texas Statutes Annotated
Tex. Rev. Civ. Stat. Ann.	Texas Revised Civil Statutes Annotated
U.S.C.	United States Code
U.S.C.A.	United States Code Annotated
U.S.C.S.	United States Code Service
Utah Code Ann.	Utah Code Annotated
Va. Code	Code of Virginia Annotated
Vt. Stat. Ann.	Vermont Statutes Annotated
Wash. Rev. Code	Revised Code of Washington
Wash. Rev. Code Ann.	Revised Code of Washington Annotated
Wis. Stat.	Wisconsin Statutes
Wis. Stat. Ann.	Wisconsin Statutes Annotated
W.Va. Code Ann.	West Virginia Code Annotated
Wyom. Stat. Ann.	Wyoming Statutes Annotated

Appendix B

State Subject Codes

Abbreviation	*Subject Code*
California	
Agric.	Agricultural
Bus. & Prof.	Business and Professions
Civ.	Civil
Civ. Proc.	Civil Procedure
Com.	Commercial
Corp.	Corporations
Educ.	Education
Elec.	Elections
Evid.	Evidence
Fin.	Financial
Fish & Game	Fish and Game
Food & Agric.	Food and Agricultural
Gov.	Government
Harb. & Nav.	Harbors and Navigation
Health & Safety	Health and Safety
Ins.	Insurance
Lab.	Labor
Mil. & Vet.	Military and Veterans
Penal	Penal
Prob.	Probate
Pub. Con.	Public Contract
Pub. Res.	Public Resources
Pub. Util.	Public Utilities
Rev. & T.	Revenue and Taxation
Str. & H.	Streets and Highways
Un. Ins.	Unemployment Insurance
Veh.	Vehicle
Water	Water
Welf. & Inst.	Welfare and Institutions

Maryland

Com. Law	Commercial Law
Const.	Constitutions
Corps. & Ass'ns	Corporations and Associations
Cts. & Jud. Proc.	Courts and Judicial Proceedings
Educ.	Education
Env.	Environmental
Est. & Trusts	Estates and Trusts
Fam. Law	Family Law
Fin. Inst.	Financial Institutions
Health Env.	Health—Environmental
Health Gen.	Health—General
Health Occ.	Health Occupations
Nat. Res.	Natural Resources
Real Prop.	Real Property
St. Fin. & Proc.	State Finance and Procurement
State Gov't	State Government
Tax Gen.	Tax—General
Transp.	Transportation

New York

Aband. Prop.	Abandoned Property
Agric. Conserv. & Adj.	Agricultural Conservation and Adjustment
Agric. & Mkts.	Agriculture and Markets
Alco. Bev. Cont.	Alcoholic Beverage Control
Alt. County Gov't	Alternative County Government
Arts & Cult. Aff.	Arts and Cultural Affairs
Banking	Banking
Ben. Ord.	Benevolent Orders
Bus. Corp.	Business Corporation
Canal	Canal
Civ. Prac. Law & R.	Civil Practice Law and Rules
Civ. Rights	Civil Rights
Civ. Serv.	Civil Service
Com.	Commerce
Condem.	Condemnation
Const.	Constitution
Coop. Corp.	Cooperative Corporations

Correct.	Corrections
County	County
Crim. Proc.	Criminal Procedure
Debt. & Cred.	Debtor and Creditor
Dom. Rel.	Domestic Relations
Econ. Dev.	Economic Development
Educ.	Education
Elec.	Election
Em. Dom. Proc.	Eminent Domain Procedure
Empl'rs Liab.	Employers' Liability
Energy	Energy
Envtl. Conserv.	Environmental Conservation
Est. Powers & Trust	Estates, Powers, and Trusts
Exec.	Executive
Gen. Ass'ns	General Associations
Gen. Bus.	General Business
Gen. City	General City
Gen. Constr.	General Construction
Gen. Mun.	General Municipal
Gen. Oblig.	General Obligations
High.	Highway
Jud. Ct. Acts	Judiciary—Court Acts
Indian	Indian
Ins.	Insurance
Jud.	Judiciary
Lab.	Labor
Legis.	Legislative
Lien	Lien
Local Fin.	Local Finance
Mental Hyg.	Mental Hygiene
Mil.	Military
Mult. Dwell.	Multiple Dwelling
Mult. Resid.	Multiple Residence
Mun. Home Rule	Municipal Home Rule
Nav.	Navigation
Not-For-Profit Corp.	Not-For-Profit Corporation
Opt. County Gov.	Optional County Government
PRHPL	Parks, Recreation, and Historical Preservation
Partnership	Partnership

Penal	Penal
Pers. Prop.	Personal Property
Priv. Hous. Fin.	Private Housing Finance
Pub. Auth.	Public Authorities
Pub. Bldgs.	Public Buildings
Pub. Health	Public Health
Pub. Hous.	Public Housing
Pub. Lands	Public Lands
Pub. Off.	Public Officers
Pub. Serv.	Public Service
RPWB	Racing, Pari-Mutuel Wagering, and Breeding
Rapid Trans.	Rapid Transit
Real Prop.	Real Property
RPAPL	Real Property Actions and Proceedings
Real Prop. Tax	Real Property Tax
Relig. Corp.	Religious Corporations
Retire. & Soc. Sec.	Retirement and Social Security
R.R.	Railroad
Rural Elec. Coop.	Rural Electric Cooperative
Salt Springs	Salt Springs
Second Class Cities	Second Class Cities
Soc. Serv.	Social Service
Soil Conserv. Dist.	Soil Conservation Districts
State	State
St. Adm. Proc. Act	State Administrative Procedure Act
State Fin.	State Finance
State Print. & Pub. Doc.	State Printing and Public Documents
Stat. Local Gov'ts	Statute of Local Governments
Surr. Ct. Proc. Act	Surrogate's Court Procedure Act
Tax	Tax
Town	Town
Transp.	Transportation
Transp. Corp.	Transportations Corporations
U.C.C.	Uniform Commercial Code
Uncons. Laws	Unconsolidated Laws
Veh. & Traf.	Vehicle and Traffic
Village	Village
Vol. Fire. Ben.	Volunteer Firemen's Benefit

Work. Comp.	Workmen's Compensation

Texas

Agric.	Agriculture
Alco. Bev.	Alcoholic Beverage
Bus. & Com.	Business and Commerce
Civ. Prac. & Rem.	Civil Practice and Remedies
Corp. & Ass'ns	Corporations and Associations
Crim. Proc.	Criminal Procedure
Educ.	Education
Elec.	Election
Fam.	Family
Fin.	Financial
Gov.	Government
Health & Safety	Health and Safety
High.	Highway
Hum. Res.	Human Resources
Ins.	Insurance
Lab.	Labor
Loc. Gov.	Local Government
Nat. Res.	Natural Resources
Occ.	Occupations
Parks & Wild.	Parks and Wildlife
Penal	Penal
Prob.	Probate
Prop.	Property
Res.	Resources
Tax	Tax
Util.	Utilities
Veh.	Vehicles
Water	Water
Welf.	Welfare

Appendix C

Common Legal Abbrevations
and Their Full Titles

Abbreviation	*Full Title*
A., A.2d	Atlantic Reporter
Ala.	Alabama Reports
Ala. App.	Alabama Appellate Court Reports
Alaska	Alaska Reports
Ariz.	Arizona Reports
Ariz. App.	Arizona Appeals Reports
Ark.	Arkansas Reports
Cal., Cal.2d, Cal.3d	California Reports
Cal. Rptr.	West's California Reporter
C.F.R.	Code of Federal Regulations
Colo.	Colorado Reports
Colo. App.	Colorado Court of Appeals Reports
Conn.	Connecticut Reports
Conn. Supp.	Connecticut Supplement
Del.	Delaware Reports
F., F.2d	Federal Reporter
Fed. Reg.	Federal Register
Fla.	Florida Reports
Fla. Supp.	Florida Supplement
F. Supp.	Federal Supplement
Ga.	Georgia Reports
Ga. App.	Georgia Appeals Reports
Hawaii	Hawaii Reports
Idaho	Idaho Reports
Ill., Ill.2d	Illinois Reports
Ill. App., Ill. App.2d	Illinois Appellate Court Reports

Ind.	Indiana Reports
Ind. App.	Indiana Court of Appeals Reports
Iowa	Iowa Reports
Kan.	Kansas Reports
Kan. App., Kan. App.2d	Kansas Court of Appeals Reports
Ky.	Kentucky Reports
La.	Louisiana Reports
Mass.	Massachusetts Reports
Mass. App. Ct.	Massachusetts Appeals Court Reports
Mass. App. Dec.	Appellate Decisions
Me.	Maine Reports
Md.	Maryland Reports
Md. App.	Maryland Appellate Reports
Mich.	Michigan Reports
Mich. App.	Michigan Appeals Reports
Minn.	Minnesota Reports
Miss.	Mississippi Reports
Mo.	Missouri Reports
Mo. App.	Missouri Appeals Reports
Mont.	Montana Reports
N.C.	North Carolina Reports
N.C. Ct. App.	North Carolina Court of Appeals Reports
N.D.	North Dakota Reports
N.E., N.E.2d	North Eastern Reporter
Neb.	Nebraska Reports
Nev.	Nevada Reports
N.H.	New Hampshire Reports
N.J.	New Jersey Reports
N.J. Super.	New Jersey Superior Court Reports
N.M.	New Mexico Reports
N.W., N.W.2d	North Western Reporter
N.Y., N.Y.2d	New York Reports
N.Y.S., N.Y.S.2d	West's New York Supplement
Ohio App., Ohio App.2d	Ohio Appellate Reports
Ohio Misc.	Ohio Miscellaneous
Ohio St., Ohio St.2d	Ohio State Reports
Okla.	Oklahoma Reports

Or.	Oregon Reports
Or. App.	Oregon Reports, Court of Appeals
P., P.2d	Pacific Reporter
Pa.	Pennsylvania State Reports
P.R.	Puerto Rico Reports
P.R. Dec.	Decisiones de Puerto Rico
R.I.	Rhode Island Reports
S.C.	South Carolina Reports
S. Ct.	Supreme Court Reporter
S.D.	South Dakota Reports
S.E., S.E.2d	South Eastern Reporter
So., So.2d	Southern Reporter
S.W., S.W.2d	South Western Reporter
Tenn.	Tennessee Reports
Tenn. App.	Tennessee Appeals
Tex.	Texas Reports
Treas. Reg.	Treasury Regulations
U.S.	United States Reports
U.S. App. D.C.	United States Court of Appeals Reports
U.S.C.	United States Code
U.S.C.A.	United States Code Annotated
U.S.L.W.	United States Law Week
Utah	Utah Reports
Vt.	Vermont Reports
Va.	Virginia Reports
Wash., Wash.2d	Washington Reports
Wash. App.	Washington Appellate Reports
W. Va.	West Virginia Reports
Wis., Wis.2d	Wisconsin Reports
Wyo.	Wyoming Reports

Appendix D

Dog Bite Statutes

Alabama
Ala. Code
Title 3, Animals

§3-1-1:
Keeping of dog known to kill, etc., stock prohibited; liability of owner for injuries, etc., caused by same; liability for killing of same

§3-1-2:
Liability of owner, etc., for injuries caused by rabid dog

§3-1-3:
Liability of owner, etc., permitting vicious or dangerous animal to be at liberty, etc., for injuries caused by same

§3-1-6:
Liability of owner, etc., for injuries to livestock, etc., caused by dog while off premises of owner, etc.

§3-6-1:
Liability of owner of a dog for injuries to person bitten or injured while upon property owned or controlled by owner, etc.

§3-6-2:
When person deemed lawfully on property of owner of dog

§3-6-3:
Mitigation of damages

§3-6-4:
Construction of chapter

Arizona
Ariz. Rev. Stat.
Title 24, Livestock and Animals
§24-361:
Definitions

§24-378:	Dogs; liability
§24-521:	Liability for dog bites
§24-522:	Lawful presence on private property defined
§24-523:	Provocation as defense
§24-524:	Dogs killing or chasing livestock; liability of owner

Arkansas
Ark. Stat. Ann.
Title 20, Public Health and Welfare

| §20-19-102: | Injuries to sheep or goats by dog |

California
Cal. Civ. Code

§3340:	Injuries to animals; exemplary damages
§3341:	Liability of owner, possessor, or harborer of animal killing or injuring other animals; scienter: right to kill animal found committing injury; accidental killing or injury
§3342:	Dog bite; liability of owner; military or police work excluded; limitations
§3342.5:	Duty of owner; action; dogs trained to fight, attack, or kill; legislation by city and county

Connecticut
Conn. Gen. Stat. Ann.
Title 22, Agriculture, Domestic Animals

§22-355:	Damage by dogs to domestic animals
§22-356:	Damage by two or more dogs
§22-357:	Damage to person or property
§22-358:	Killing of dogs doing damage
§22-362:	Annoyance of dogs on highways
§22-363:	Nuisance
§22-367:	General penalty. Enforcement

Delaware
Del. Code Ann.
Title 7, Conservation
§1704:   Dogs running at large
§1711:   Liability of dog owners in civil action;
                                payment from licensing funds
§1716:   Confinement of biting dogs; notice to
                                local health authority; exemption

District of Columbia
D.C. Code
Title 6, Health and Safety
§6-1001:   Definitions
§6-1011:   Penalty
§6-1011:   Notice of violation
§6-1012:   Civil Liability

Florida
Fla. Stat.
Title 45, Torts
§767.01:   Dog owner's liability for damages to
                                persons or domestic animals
§767.04:   Dog owner's liability for damages to
                                persons bitten
§767.05:   Dog owner's liability for damages by dog
                                that kills, wounds, or harasses dairy
                                cattle

Georgia
Ga. Code Ann.
Title 4, Animals
§4-8-4:   Liability of owner, etc., for damages
                                done to livestock or poultry by dog
§4-8-7:   Penalty for violations of chapter

Hawaii
Hawaii Rev. Stat.
Title 11, Agriculture and Animals
§142-74:   Liability of dog owner; penalty

§142-75:   Human bitten by dog; duty of dog owners; action against owner

Title 36, Civil Remedies and Defenses and Special Proceedings

§663-9:   Liability of animal owners

§663-9.1:   Exception of animal owners to civil liability

Idaho
Idaho Code
Title 25, Animals

§25-2806:   Liability for livestock and poultry killed by dogs

§25-2808:   Dogs used in law enforcement

Illinois
Ill. Rev. Stat.
Title 8, Animals

§369:   Reimbursement of owner of domestic animals killed or injured by dog

§352.16:   Owner

§366:   Liability of owner of dog attacking or injuring person

§368:   Killing of dog seen to injure, wound, or kill domestic animals

§370:   Payment to owner of domestic animals no bar to action for damages— Repayment to animal control fund

Indiana
Ind. Code Ann.
Title 15, Agriculture and Animals

§15-5-7-1:   Liability of owner or harborer

§15-5-12-1:   Dog bite liability

Iowa
Iowa Code Ann.
Title 14, County and Township Government

§351.2:   "Owner" defined

§351.28:   Liability for damages

Kentucky
Ky. Rev. Stat.

Title 21, Agriculture and Animals
§258.095:   Definitions
§258.235:   Authority to kill dog—Proceeding by
                    person attacked by dog—Vicious dog
                    not to run at large
§258.275:   Liability for property loss or injury by
                    dog or coyote—Procedure for enforcing
                    claims for damages
§258.285:   Payment from livestock fund—
                    Subrogation of claimant's rights
§258.295:   Payment by dog owner bars payment
                    from livestock fund—Maximum sums
                    for certain livestock and poultry—
                    Appraisals to be of actual value
§258.325:   Confinement and destruction of dog
                    found to have caused loss or damage to
                    livestock, persons or poultry—Harborer
                    of unlicensed dog forfeits rights in
                    livestock fund
§258.345:   Quarantine of dogs in case of excessive
                    damage to livestock, poultry or domestic
                    game birds

Louisiana
La. Civ. Code
Title 5, Offenses and Quasi-Offenses
§2321:   Damage Caused by Animals

Maine
Me. Rev. Stat. Ann.
Title 7, Agriculture and Animals
§3961:   Reimbursement for damage done by
                    dogs
§3962:   Complaint and recovery
§3963:   Joint and several liability
§3964:   Damage by animals

Maryland
Md. Ann. Code
Title 56, Licenses

Michigan
Mich. Comp. Laws Ann.
Chapter 287, Agriculture—Animal Industry

§287.261:   Short title; definitions
§287.279:   Dogs pursuing livestock or poultry,
                     attacking persons, or entering livestock
                     or poultry producer's field
§287.280:   Damage to livestock or poultry by dogs,
                     remedy; complaint, proceedings;
                     liability for damages and costs
§287.282:   Same; fees of justice, inclusion in
                     damages
§287.283:   Payment by county for damage done by
                     dogs; illegal or unjust claim,
                     investigation
§287.284:   Reception, audit, determination, and
                     payment of damage claims; board of
                     county auditors
§287.351:   Dog, injury by; liability of owner

Minnesota
Minn. Stat. Ann.
Chapter 374, Dogs

§347.01:   Owner's liability; penalty
§347.02:   Keeping after notice; penalty
§347.04:   Public nuisance
§347.15:   Persons damaged, claims filed
§347.16:   Claims, hearings, notice
§347.22:   Damages, owner liability

Mississippi
Miss. Code Ann.
Title 95, Torts

§95-5-21:   Poultry and livestock killed by dog—
                     owner liable

Missouri
Mo. Ann. Stat.
Title 17, Agriculture and Animals

§273.020:   Recovery of damages for sheep killed—disposition of dog; penalty

§273.110:   Application to recover damages from fund

Montana
Mont. Code Ann.
Title 27, Civil Liability, Remedies, and Limitations
§27-1-715:   Liability of owner of vicious dog

Nebraska
Neb. Rev. Stat.
Title 54, Livestock
§54-601:   Dogs; personal property; owner liability for damages

§54-602:   Dogs owned by different persons; joint liability

Nevada
Nev. Rev. Stat.
Title 15, Crimes and Punishments
§202.500:   Unlawful to keep vicious dog
Title 50, Animals
§568.370:   Permitting dogs to chase, worry, injure or kill domestic animals on open range or private property unlawful

New Hampshire
N.H. Rev. Stat. Ann.
Title 45, Animals
§466:19:   Liability of owner or keeper
§466:20:   Double damages
§466:21:   Liability of towns or cities
§466:22:   Procedure to enforce
§466:25:   Orders, how payable
§466:27:   Election of remedy
§466:31:   Dogs a menace, a nuisance or vicious
§466:31a: Penalties
§46:32:   Officers' fees
§466:34:   Pursuing game, etc.

§466:35:   Maiming game
§466:38:   How recoverable

New Jersey
N.J. Stat. Ann.
Title 4, Agriculture and Domestic Animals
§4:15-1:   Definitions
§4:19-4:   Use of tax collections to pay claims; handling of fund
§4:19-5:   Claims for and establishment of damages
§4:19-6:   Suit by municipality against owner
§4:19-7:   Effect of article on owner's liability
§4:19-8:   Failure to kill dog found worrying animals or poultry; penalty; triple damages
§4:19-16:   Liability of owner regardless of viciousness of dog

New Mexico
N.M. Stat. Ann.
Chapter 77, Animals and Animal Industry
§77-1-2:   Dog killing or injuring livestock; damages; dog to be killed

New York
N.Y. Agric. & Mkts. Law
§121:   Dangerous dogs
§125:   Indemnification for dog damage
§188:   Definitions

North Carolina
N.C. Gen. Stat.
Chapter 67, Dogs
§67-1:   Liability for injury to livestock or fowls
§67-12:   Permitting dogs to run at large at night; penalty; liability for damage

North Dakota
N.D. Cent. Code
Title 36, Livestock

| §36-21-11: | Owners of dogs liable for damages done to livestock—Procedure when damages done by pack of dogs |

Title 42, Nuisances

| §42-03-01: | When dogs are a public nuisance |

Ohio
Ohio Rev. Code Ann.
Title 9, Agriculture—Animals—Fences

§955.26.1:	Duties after dog bites person; quarantine
§955.28:	Dog may be killed for certain acts; owner liable for damages
§955.29:	Claim of owner
§955.30:	Action to recover for loss
§955.31:	Additional information
§955.32:	Registered stock
§955.33:	Hearing
§955.34:	Witnesses
§955.35:	Payment of claims

Oklahoma
Okla. Stat. Ann.
Title 4, Animals

§41:	Dogs chasing or worrying sheep, other livestock or poultry—Right to kill—Liability for damages—Nuisance
§42.1:	Personal injury by dog—Liability of owner
§42.2:	Lawful presence on owner's property, what constitutes—Public place, what is
§42.3:	Exceptions to application of act—Existing rights and liabilities

Oregon
Or. Rev. Stat.
Title 48, Animals

| §609.090: | Impounding certain dogs; disposing of dogs; fees for impoundment; release of dog |
| §609.095: | Dog as public nuisance; public nuisance |

§4-13-17:	Civil liability of person harboring dog for damages
§4-13-20:	Appraisal of damages done by dogs—Payment from town treasury—Excepted towns and cities
§4-13-21:	Appraisal and payment of damages in certain Newport county towns
§4-13-22:	Subrogation of town or city to claim for damages

South Carolina
S.C. Code Ann.
Title 47, Animals, Livestock and Poultry

§47-3-110:	Liability of owner or person having dog in his care or keeping
§47-3-230:	Liability of owner of sheep-killing dog for payment to owner of sheep killed or injured
§47-3-320:	Training of conservation officers to remove dogs; liability of officials

South Dakota
S.D. Codified Laws Ann.
Title 40, Animals and Livestock

§40-34-2:	Liability of owner for damages by dog disturbing domestic animals—Property subject to execution
§40-34-3:	Joint liability of owners for damages by dogs in packs—Rights of contribution among dog owners
§40-34-4:	Dogs at large declared nuisance by county commissioners—Abatement
§40-34-15:	Injury to person trespassing, teasing dog, or attempting to commit crime

Tennessee
Tenn. Code Ann.
Title 44, Animals and Animal Husbandry

| §44-17-120: | Destruction of dog causing death or serious injury to human—Notice to |

	dog's owner
§44-17-201:	Owners of dogs are liable for livestock killed
§44-17-202:	Ignorance of dog's habits is no defense

Texas
Tex. Rev. Civ. Stat. Ann.
Title 7, Animals

| §192-4: | Destruction of dog causing death of person |

Utah
Utah Code Ann.
Title 18, Dogs

| §18-1-1: | Liability of owners—scienter—Dogs used in law enforcement |
| §18-1-2: | Dogs acting together—Actions—Parties—Judgment |

Vermont
Vt. Stat. Ann.
Title 20, Internal Security and Public Safety

§3741:	Election of remedy
§3742:	Notice of damage; appraisal
§3746:	Action against town
§3747:	Action by town against owner of dogs
§3748:	Action by sheep owner against dog owner

Virginia
Va. Code
Title 3.1, Agriculture, Horticulture and Food

§3.1-796.116:	Dogs killing, injuring or chasing livestock or poultry
§3.1-796.117:	Dog killing domestic animals other than livestock or poultry
§3.1-796.118:	Compensation for livestock and poultry killed by dogs

DOGS AND THE LAW

Wyoming
Wyo. Stat. Ann.
Title 11, Agriculture and Animals
§11-31-105:   Killing sheep or other domestic animals;
                liability of owner
§11-31-106:   Same; destruction
§11-31-208:   Reimbursement for loss of livestock
                from license fund; procedure

Appendix E

Small Claims Courts:
Jurisdictional Limits

State	Citation	Dollar Amount
Alabama	Ala. Code §12-12-31	$1,000
Alaska	Alaska Stat. §22-15.040	5,000*
Arizona	Ariz. Rev. Stat. Ann. §22-201	500
Arkansas	Ark. Code Ann. §16-17-704	3,000
California	Cal. Civ. Proc. Code §116.2	2,000
		2,500
		eff. 1/1/91
Colorado	Colo. Rev. Stat. Ann. §13-6-403	2,000*
Connecticut	Conn. Gen. Stat. Ann. §51-15	1,500
Delaware	Unavailable	
District of Columbia	D.C. Code Ann. §11-1321	2,000*
Florida	Fla. Stat. Ann. §34.01	5,000*
Georgia	Ga. Code Ann art. 6 §3	200
Hawaii	Hawaii Rev. Stat. §633-27	2,500*
Idaho	Idaho Code §1-2301	2,000*
Illinois	Ill. Ann. Stat. ch. 110A §281	2,500
Indiana	Ind. Code Ann. §33-11.6-4-21	3,000*
Iowa	Iowa Code Ann. §631.1	2,000*
Kansas	Kan. Stat. Ann. §61-2703	1,000

Kentucky	Ky. Rev. Stat. Ann. §24A:230	1,500*
Louisiana	La. Rev. Stat. Ann. §13:5202	2,000*
Maine	Me. Rev. Stat. Ann. tit. 14 §7482	1,400*
Maryland	Md. Ann. Code §4-405	2,500*
Massachusetts	Mass. Gen. Laws Ann. ch. 21 §21	1,500
Michigan	Mich. Comp. Laws Ann. §600.6419	1,000*
Minnesota	Minn. Stat. Ann. §488.04	1,000
Mississippi	Miss. Code Ann. §9-11-9	1,000
Missouri	Mo. Ann. Stat. §482.305	1,500*
Montana	Mont. Code Ann. §25-34-102	1,500
Nebraska	Neb. Rev. Stat. §2654-522	1,500*
Nevada	Nev. Rev. Stat. Ann. §73.010	1,500
New Hampshire	N.H. Rev. Stat. Ann. §503.1	1,500*
New Jersey	N.J. Stat. Ann. §2A:6-43	1,000*
New Mexico	N.M. Stat. Ann. §34-8A-3	5,000
New York	N.Y. Judiciary-Court Acts Law	2,000*
North Carolina	N.C. Gen. Stat. Ann. §7A-210	1,500
North Dakota	N.D. Cent. Code Ann. § 27-08.1-01	2,000
Ohio	Ohio Rev. Code Ann. §1925.02	1,000*
Oklahoma	Okla. Stat. Ann. tit. 12 §1754	1,500
Oregon	Or. Rev. Stat. §46.405	200
Pennsylvania	Pa. Cons. Stat. Ann. tit. 42 §1123	5,000*
Puerto Rico	Laws of P.R. Ann. T.32APPIII Rule 60	500
Rhode Island	R.I. Gen. Laws §10-16-1	1,500*
South Carolina	S.C. Code Ann. §22-3-10	2,500
South Dakota	S.D. Codified Laws §15-39-45	2,000*
Tennessee	Unavailable	
Texas	Tex. Civ. Code Ann. §28.003	1,000
Utah	Utah Code Ann. §78-6-1	1,000*
Vermont	Vt. Stat. Ann. tit. 12 §5531	2,000*
Virginia	Va. Code Ann. §16-1-122.2	1,000*
Washington	Wash. Rev. Code Ann. §12:40.010	2,000
West Virginia	Unavailable	
Wisconsin	Wis. Stat. Ann. §799.01(4)	2,000
Wyoming	Wyo. Stat. Ann. §1-21-201	2,000

*Excludes costs and interest

Index

CAVEAT

This book is written merely as a general survey of the laws pertaining to dogs. The laws vary tremendously from jurisdiction to jurisdiction. They also change over time and are subject to the interpretation of the controlling authorities.

Any reference to a resource material or facility is not an endorsement.

DOGS
AND THE LAW

By Anmarie Barrie, esq.